Explore new ideas!

MW01591166

Think It Through

Read exciting literature, science and social studies texts!

Become an expert writer!

Build vocabulary and knowledge to unlock the Wonders of reading!

Use your student login to explore your interactive Reading/Writing Workshop, practice close reading, and more.

Go Digital! www.connected.mcgraw-hill.com

(tl) imac/Alamy; (rb) Stephen Frink/Corbis; (rt) R.G. Roth; (b) Nathan Love

Cover and Title Pages: Nathan Love

www.mheonline.com/readingwonders

Copyright © 2017 McGraw-Hill Education

Send all inquiries to:
McGraw-Hill Education
2 Penn Plaza
New York, NY 10121

ISBN: 978-0-07-898093-0
MHID: 0-07-898093-3

Printed in the United States of America

1 2 3 4 5 6 7 8 9 LWI 22 21 20 19 18 17

A

Wonders

An English Language Arts Program

Program Authors

Diane August

Donald R. Bear

Janice A. Dole

Jana Echevarria

Douglas Fisher

David Francis

Vicki Gibson

Jan Hasbrouck

Margaret Kilgo

Jay McTighe

Scott G. Paris

Timothy Shanahan

Josefina V. Tinajero

Mc
Graw
Hill
Education

Unlock the
Wonders
of
Reading

With your *Reading/Writing Workshop* you will:

- Closely read and reread literature and informational text

- Discuss what you have read with your peers

- Become a better writer and researcher

- Look for text evidence as you respond to complex text

Get Ready to Become:

- Lifelong Learners
- Critical Thinkers
- Part of the Community of Learning

READ and REREAD

Exciting Literature

Open your book and fire up your imagination! You'll find myths, fables, stories, poems, and dramas. They're all there waiting for you to explore and share.

Informational Texts

Build knowledge with many kinds of informational texts. Sometimes the real world is more exciting than fiction.

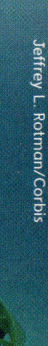

ACT
Access Complex Text

Different kinds of texts can be challenging. First you need to figure out why the text is hard for you. Once you determine what the difficulty is, you can try to solve it. Look at the tips below. They can help you move in the right direction.

VOCABULARY

If you come across an unfamiliar word, look for context clues. Some texts contain technical terms. You might want to look these up in a dictionary.

MAKE CONNECTIONS

Sometimes you may need to make inferences about the text. For example, the reasons a character does something are not always stated. In nonfiction you can connect information to find the essential idea.

ILLUSTRATIONS AND TEXT FEATURES

Are there any illustrations that can give you clues about the plot or how the characters feel? In nonfiction, are there any maps or diagrams that can help you understand information in the text?

TEXT STRUCTURE

How is the text organized? Does the author compare and contrast information? Is there a series of problems presented? Are there steps in a process?

. . . .

COLLABORATE

How might a chart or graph help you understand information in a nonfiction text?

L👀K for Text Evidence

When you answer a question about your reading, you often have to look for evidence in the text to support or even find the answer. Here are some tips to help you find what you are looking for.

Once upon a time, long before computers, baseball, or pizza, there lived a young man named Liang. During the day, **Liang helped his father build furniture.**

Stated

Here I can locate specific information that tells me what Liang helped his father build.

At dinner that night, Liang told his father that he wanted to marry Princess Peng. His father almost **choked on the stale, hard rice ball he was eating.**

A year later, Liang and Princess Peng were married. They opened a toy shop together and lived happily ever after.

Unstated

This text evidence allows me to make the inference that Liang's father is in shock.

Text Evidence

Evidence will either be stated or implied. If it is implied, it means that it is not directly stated in the text. Here's how to tell if a question will have a stated or an unstated answer.

It's Stated - Right There!

The answers to questions that ask you to find a certain fact, event, or setting can usually be found in a single sentence.

To answer other questions you need to combine stated information from more than one place. A question such as, "What steps does Liang take to try to marry the Princess?" means you have to look in the beginning, middle, and end of the text.

It's Unstated - Here is My Evidence

The answers to some questions are not stated. These kinds of questions ask you to analyze information, put the answer in your own words, and support it with text evidence.

How do you look for text evidence? For theme, think about what the characters do and say. In a nonfiction text, look for signal words and phrases.

· ·

Point to stated information that tells when this story took place.

Be an Expert Writer

Remember that good writing presents clear ideas, is well organized, and contains evidence and details from reliable sources. See how Zoe answered a question about a text she read.

Zoe's Model

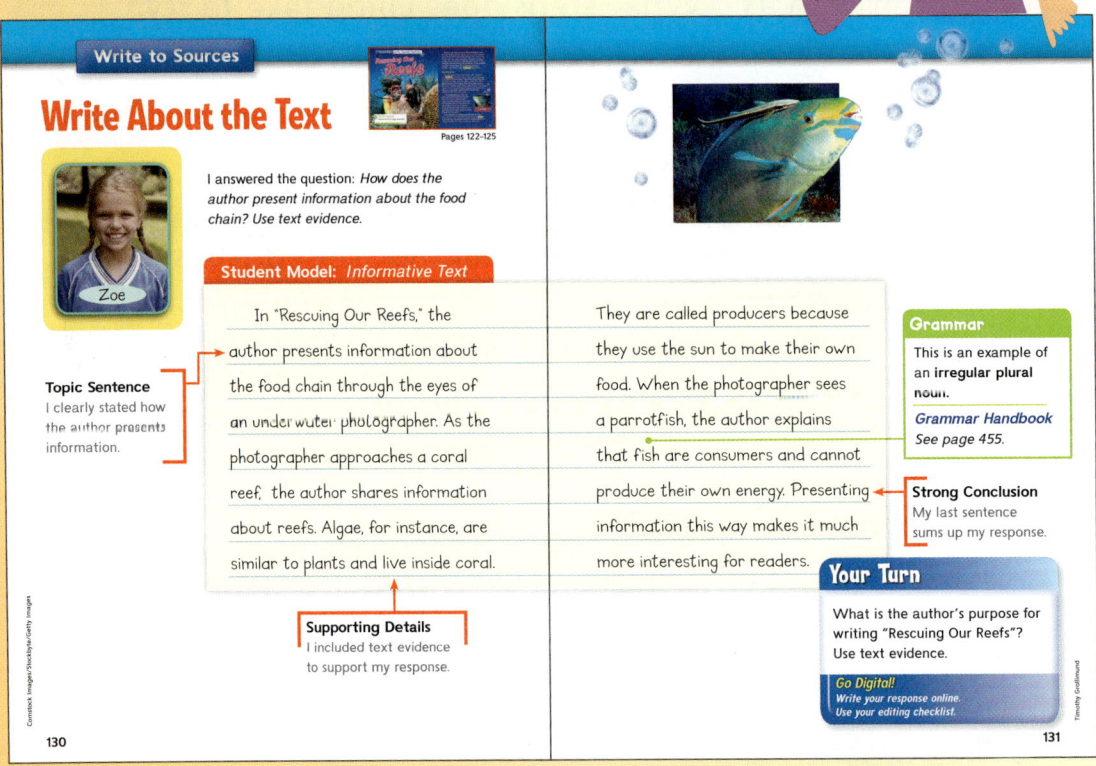

Write to Sources

Write About the Text

Pages 122-125

I answered the question: *How does the author present information about the food chain? Use text evidence.*

Student Model: *Informative Text*

Zoe

Topic Sentence
I clearly stated how the author presents information.

In "Rescuing Our Reefs," the author presents information about the food chain through the eyes of an underwater photographer. As the photographer approaches a coral reef, the author shares information about reefs. Algae, for instance, are similar to plants and live inside coral.

They are called producers because they use the sun to make their own food. When the photographer sees a parrotfish, the author explains that fish are consumers and cannot produce their own energy. Presenting information this way makes it much more interesting for readers.

Supporting Details
I included text evidence to support my response.

Grammar
This is an example of an **irregular plural noun.**
Grammar Handbook
See page 455.

Strong Conclusion
My last sentence sums up my response.

Your Turn
What is the author's purpose for writing "Rescuing Our Reefs"? Use text evidence.
Go Digital!
Write your response online. Use your editing checklist.

Comstock Images/Stockbyte/Getty Images

Timothy Gröllmund

130

131

Write About the Text

When you write about something you have read closely, you should introduce your topic clearly. Cite evidence from the text that supports your opinions. When you do research, make sure you use multiple reliable sources and then provide a list of the sources you have used. Use the question checklist below.

Opinions Did I support opinions with facts and details?

Informative Texts Did I clearly group information in paragraphs? Did I make a closing statement connecting all of my information?

Narrative Texts When you write a narrative, you use your imagination to develop real or made-up events. The checklist below will help make your stories memorable.

- **Sequence** Did I use a sequence of events that unfolds naturally? Did I make use of clue words and phrases?

- **Dialogue** Did I use dialogue and description to develop characters, experiences, and events? Do I show the responses of characters to situations?

 What is your favorite thing to write about? Tell a partner why.

Unit 1

Think It Through

The Big Idea

How can a challenge bring out our best?...... **16**

(t) Alessandra Cimatoribus; (c) Valerie Sokolova; (b) Chris Vallo

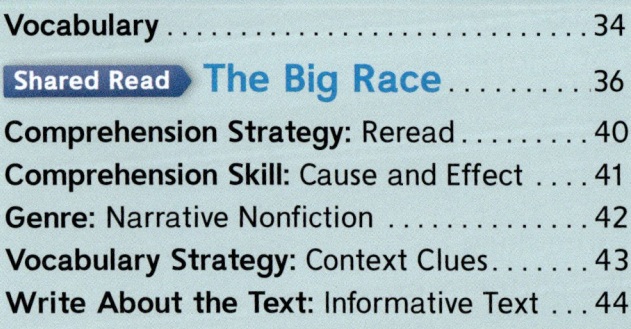

Go Digital! www.connected.mcgraw-hill.com.

(t) Westend61/Getty Images; (c) Craig Phillips

Think It Through

The BIG Idea

How can a challenge bring out our best?

The Crow and the Pitcher

A thirsty crow was flying high above the hot, dry desert when she spied a broken pitcher. The top was sharp and jagged, but she saw that there was water in the bottom. She poked her beak into the pitcher but could not reach the water so she picked up a pebble and threw it at the pitcher hoping to smash it. The pebble fell into the pitcher, hitting the water with a plop.

The angry crow picked up another pebble and was about to throw it when she stopped. She flew to the pitcher and dropped the pebble inside.

Plop!

She dropped another pebble, and another, and another.

Plop! Plop! Plop!

With each pebble the water rose closer to the top. Soon the crow was able to drink the water.

Alessandra Cimatoribus

17

? How do people respond to natural disasters?

Go Digital!

To the Rescue

Natural disasters are events such as hurricanes, earthquakes, floods, and forest fires. When these kinds of events occur, it can cause a huge crisis in a community. Luckily, there are people who are trained to respond to natural disasters.

▶ How might people respond to a forest fire?

▶ How do you think people are rescued during a flood?

▶ What are some ways that people might respond during other kinds of natural disasters?

Talk About It

Write words you have learned about responding to natural disasters. Then talk to a partner about what you might do to help after a natural disaster.

Natural Disasters

(bkgd) Masterfile. (c) Oleksiy Maksymenko/Alamy

Vocabulary

Use the picture and the sentences to talk with a partner about each word.

alter

The ocean waves slowly **alter** the shoreline by carving away the rocks.

How can people alter their appearance?

collapse

Flood waters caused the bridge to **collapse**.

What might cause a tent to collapse?

crisis

Rescue workers help people during an emergency or a **crisis,** such as a flood.

How would you react to a crisis?

destruction

The tornado destroyed buildings and caused a lot of other **destruction**.

What is a synonym for destruction?

hazard

The water was a **hazard** to people driving on the street.

What else might be a hazard to people who are driving?

severe

Severe weather can include very strong winds and heavy rain.

Describe severe winter weather.

substantial

We got a **substantial** amount of snow last night.

What is an antonym for substantial?

unpredictable

The **unpredictable** weather turned suddenly from sun to rain.

What is an antonym for unpredictable?

COLLABORATE

Your Turn

Pick three words. Write three questions for your partner to answer.

Go Digital! *Use the online visual glossary*

A World of CHANGE

? **Inquiry Question**

How do natural forces affect us?

The Grand Canyon Skywalk, Arizona

Earth may seem as if it is a large rock that never changes. Actually, our planet is in a constant state of change. Natural changes take place every day. These activities alter the surface of Earth. Some of these changes take place slowly over many years. Others happen in just minutes. Whether they are slow or fast, both kinds of changes have a great effect on our planet.

Slow and Steady

Some of Earth's biggest changes can't be seen. That is because they are happening very slowly. Weathering, erosion, and deposition are three natural processes that change the surface of the world. They do it one grain of sand at a time.

Weathering occurs when rain, snow, sun, and wind break down rocks into smaller pieces. These tiny pieces of rock turn into soil, but they are not carried away from the landform.

Erosion occurs when weathered pieces of rock are carried away by a natural force such as a river. This causes landforms on Earth to get smaller. They may even completely collapse over time. The Grand Canyon is an example of the effect of erosion. It was carved over thousands of years by the Colorado River.

After the process of erosion, dirt and rocks are then dropped in a new location. This process is called deposition. Over time, a large collection of deposits may occur in one place. Deposition by water can build up a beach. Deposition by wind can create a substantial landform, such as a sand dune.

(bkgd) Julie Quarry/Alamy; (titles) image100/Corbis

Although erosion is a slow process, it still creates problems for people. Some types of erosion are dangerous. They can be seen as a <mark>hazard</mark> to communities.

To help protect against beach erosion, people build structures that block ocean waves from the shore. They may also use heavy rocks to keep the land from eroding. Others grow plants along the shore. The roots of the plants help hold the soil and make it less likely to erode.

Unfortunately, people cannot protect the land when fast natural processes occur.

Fast and Powerful

Fast natural processes, like slow processes, change the surface of Earth. But fast processes are much more powerful. They are often called natural disasters because of the <mark>destruction</mark> they cause. Volcanic eruptions and landslides are just two examples.

Volcanoes form around openings in Earth's crust. When pressure builds under Earth's surface, hot melted rock called magma is forced upwards. It flows up through the volcano and out through the opening. Eruptions can occur without warning. They have the potential to cause a <mark>crisis</mark> in a community.

Like volcanic eruptions, landslides can happen without warning. They occur when rocks and dirt, loosened by heavy rains, slide down a hill or mountain. Some landslides are small. Others can be quite large and cause **severe** damage.

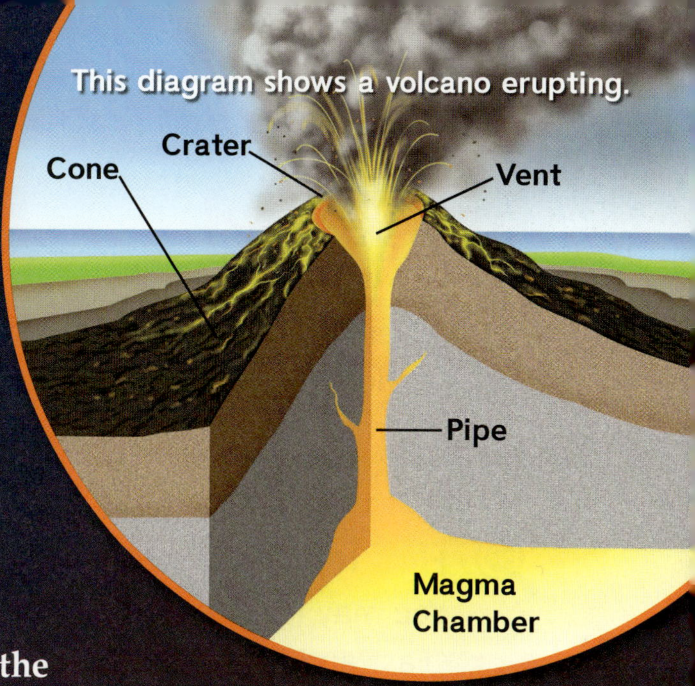

Be Prepared

In contrast to slow-moving processes, people cannot prevent the effects of fast-moving natural disasters. Instead, scientists try to predict when these events will occur so that they can warn people. Still, some disasters are **unpredictable** and strike without warning. It is important for communities to have an emergency plan in place so that they can be evacuated quickly.

The surface of Earth constantly changes through natural processes. These processes can be gradual or swift. They help to make Earth the amazing planet that it is!

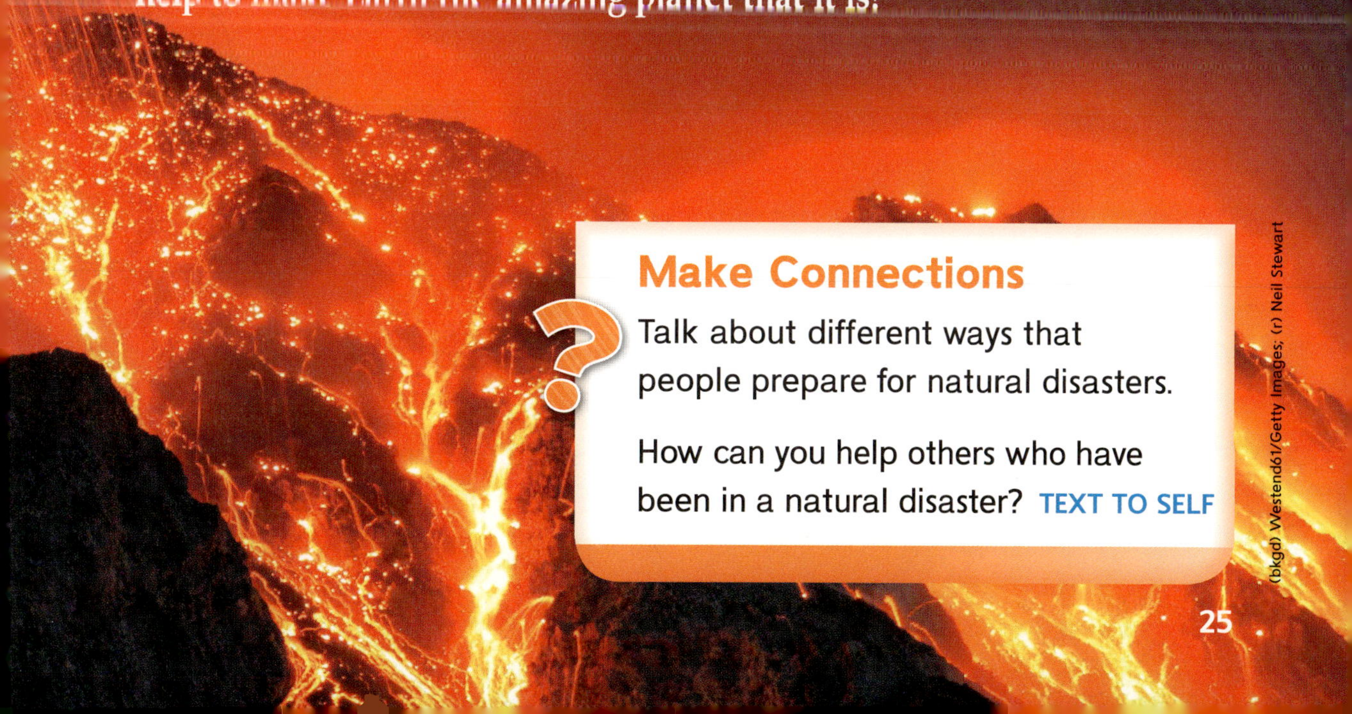

This diagram shows a volcano erupting.

Crater

Cone

Vent

Pipe

Magma Chamber

Make Connections

Talk about different ways that people prepare for natural disasters.

How can you help others who have been in a natural disaster? **TEXT TO SELF**

(bkgd) Westend61/Getty Images; (r) Neil Stewart

Reread

When you read an informational text, you may come across facts and ideas that are new to you. As you read "A World of Change," you can reread the difficult sections to make sure you understand them and to help you remember key details.

 Find Text Evidence

You may not be sure why a volcano erupts. Reread the section "Fast and Powerful" on page 24 of "A World of Change."

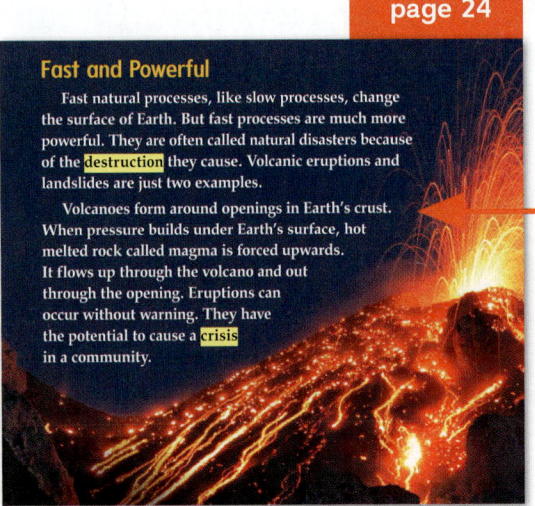

page 24

Fast and Powerful

Fast natural processes, like slow processes, change the surface of Earth. But fast processes are much more powerful. They are often called natural disasters because of the destruction they cause. Volcanic eruptions and landslides are just two examples.

Volcanoes form around openings in Earth's crust. When pressure builds under Earth's surface, hot melted rock called magma is forced upwards. It flows up through the volcano and out through the opening. Eruptions can occur without warning. They have the potential to cause a crisis in a community.

I read that when pressure builds under Earth's surface, magma is forced upwards. From this I can draw the inference that pressure below the surface causes a volcano to erupt.

COLLABORATE

Your Turn

What happens to rock during weathering? Reread the section "Slow and Steady" on page 23 to find out. As you read, remember to use the strategy Reread.

Compare and Contrast

Authors use text structure to organize the information in a text. Comparison is one kind of text structure. Authors who use this text structure show how things are alike and different.

 Find Text Evidence

Looking back at pages 23–24 of "A World of Change, " I can reread to learn how slow natural processes and fast natural processes are alike and different. Words such as some, but, both, *and* like *let me know that a comparison is being made.*

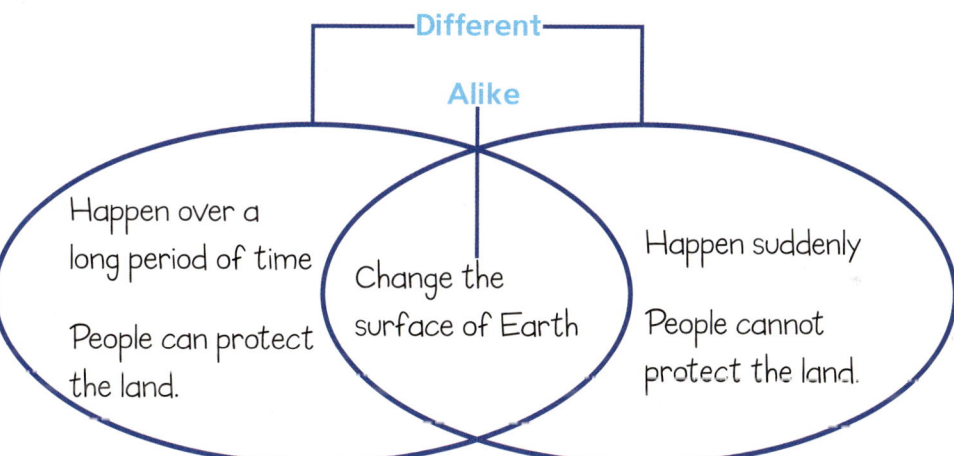

Different

Alike

Happen over a long period of time

People can protect the land.

Change the surface of Earth

Happen suddenly

People cannot protect the land.

COLLABORATE

Your Turn

Reread the section "Fast and Powerful." Compare and contrast volcanoes and landslides. List the information in the graphic organizer.

Go Digital! *Use the interactive graphic organizer*

27

Expository

The selection "A World of Change" is an expository text.

Expository text:
- Explains facts about a topic.
- Includes text features.

 ## Find Text Evidence

"A World of Change" is an expository text. It gives many facts about Earth's processes. Each section has a heading that tells me what the section is about. The diagram gives me more information.

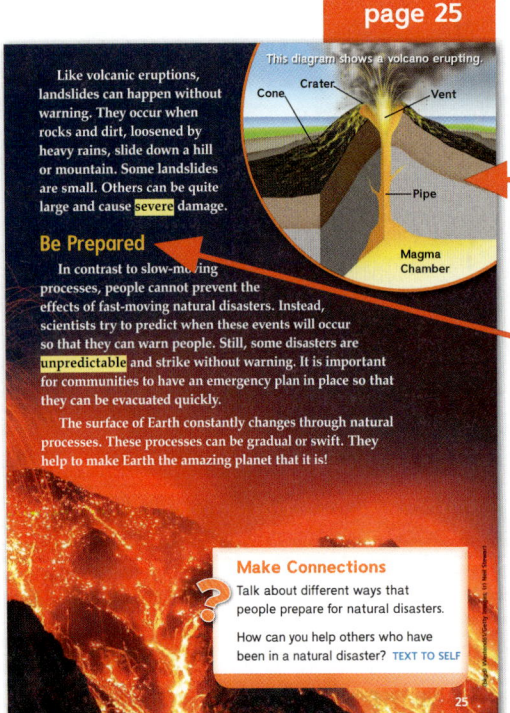

page 25

Like volcanic eruptions, landslides can happen without warning. They occur when rocks and dirt, loosened by heavy rains, slide down a hill or mountain. Some landslides are small. Others can be quite large and cause severe damage.

Be Prepared

In contrast to slow-moving processes, people cannot prevent the effects of fast-moving natural disasters. Instead, scientists try to predict when these events will occur so that they can warn people. Still, some disasters are unpredictable and strike without warning. It is important for communities to have an emergency plan in place so that they can be evacuated quickly.

The surface of Earth constantly changes through natural processes. These processes can be gradual or swift. They help to make Earth the amazing planet that it is!

This diagram shows a volcano erupting.

Cone — Crater — Vent — Pipe — Magma Chamber

Make Connections

Talk about different ways that people prepare for natural disasters.

How can you help others who have been in a natural disaster? TEXT TO SELF

25

Text Features

Diagrams Diagrams show the parts of something or how a process works. They have labels that tell about their different parts.

Headings Headings tell what a section of text is mostly about.

COLLABORATE

Your Turn

List three text features in "A World of Change." Tell your partner what information you learned from each of the features.

28

Multiple-Meaning Words

As you read "A World of Change," you will come across some **multiple-meaning words**. These are words that have more than one meaning. To figure out the meaning of a multiple-meaning word, check the words and phrases near it for clues.

 Find Text Evidence

When I read page 24 of "A World of Change," I see the word block. *There are a few different meanings for* block, *so this is a multiple-meaning word. The word* protect *and the phrase "ocean waves from the shore" help me figure out which meaning is being used in the sentence.*

To help protect against beach erosion, people build structures that block ocean waves from the shore.

Your Turn

Use context clues to figure out the meanings of the following words in "A World of Change."

place, *page 23*
shore, *page 24*
strike, *page 25*

(bc) Denis Jr. Tangney/Vetta/Getty Images

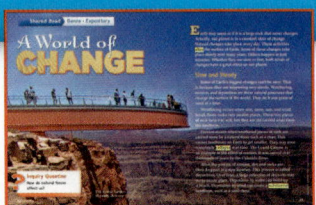

Pages 22–25

Write About the Text

Sara

I answered this question: *How does the author's use of text structure help us understand slow and fast natural processes? Use text evidence.*

Student Model: *Informative Text*

In "A World of Change," the author uses the compare and contrast text structure to help us understand slow and fast natural processes. Slow processes change the world one grain of sand at a time, but fast processes are more sudden and powerful.

Grammar

Use a comma before a conjunction in a **compound sentence**.

Grammar Handbook See page 451.

Focus on a Topic
I used facts to support the topic.

Both processes have a great effect on our planet. For example, erosion slowly carves canyons, but volcanic eruptions change the land in the blink of an eye. Comparing and contrasting the processes helps us understand the different ways the planet is shaped.

Text Structure
I included examples to show comparison.

Figurative Language
I wrote an idiom to make my point.

Your Turn

How does the use of the volcano diagram on page 25 help us to better understand the text? Use text evidence.

Go Digital!
Write your response online.
Use your editing checklist.

HOW DOES IT WORK?

Science can help us understand a lot of things—from how to throw a curve ball to what happens when you ride a roller coaster. Look at this picture. What keeps these people from falling out? Let's use science to find out!

▶ How do you stay in place during the loop-the-loops? The force created by the acceleration presses you against the seat of the coaster.

▶ What kind of rides have you ridden on at an amusement park? Why did you like them?

Talk About It

Write words that you have learned about motion. Talk to your partner about a ride that you would design.

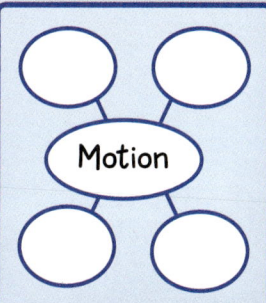

Motion

Vocabulary

Use the picture and the sentences to talk with a partner about each word.

accelerate

I saw the race car **accelerate**, or speed up, across the finish line.

What is an antonym for accelerate?

advantage

The father's size gave him a big **advantage** over his son.

What is a synonym for advantage?

capabilities

The **capabilities** of a potter include strength and creativity.

What capabilities would an athlete need?

friction

The **friction** between the tires and the pavement slows down the airplane.

How is using the brakes on a bike an example of friction?

gravity

Gravity helps pull the batter down into the baking pan.

Describe what would happen if there were no gravity on Earth.

identity

The woman showed her passport to prove her **identity**.

Why might somebody want to keep his or her identity a secret?

inquiry

Reporters ask questions at the beginning of any **inquiry** or investigation.

How are the words inquiry and investigation similar?

thrilling

Going on a roller coaster can be exciting and **thrilling**.

What is an antonym for thrilling?

Your Turn

COLLABORATE

Pick three words. Write three questions for your partner to answer.

Go Digital!   *Use the online visual glossary*

Alex and Liam planned to build a car for the soap box derby. As a result of their **inquiry** into how to build a fast car, they had come to the science museum today for answers. Last week, Alex's mother had called one of the museum's scientists. When they walked into the museum, a woman in a lab coat and inline skates zoomed up and greeted them.

"Hi, I'm Clara. Are you the boys who want to know what will make a car go fast?"

"Yes, I'm Alex, and that's Liam," Alex responded.

"Why are you wearing inline skates, Clara?" Liam asked.

"I'm a champion skater!" Clara claimed, doing a spin. Then she whispered, "That's not my true **identity**. I'm a scientist. Skates make it easier to get around. Follow me!"

IT'S ABOUT SPEED

"Welcome to our On the Move exhibit," Clara announced as they entered a large room. "So, tell me about the race."

"There will be 20 cars in the race. We'll be going down the steepest hill in town!" Alex said.

"Sounds **thrilling**! It must be exciting to go fast!" Clara answered as she pressed buttons on a machine. "This is a virtual race car, and this screen shows you the virtual race course and your speed. Speed is the distance an object moves in a certain amount of time."

Craig Phillips

37

FORCES AT WORK

Alex and Liam climbed into the machine. Each seat had a steering wheel and a screen in front of it.

A force is a push or pull.

Clara said, "Since you want to build a fast car, you need to know about forces and how they affect motion."

"What's a force?" asked Liam.

Clara continued, "A force is a push or a pull. Forces cause things to move or cause a change in motion. When I apply a big enough force on an object, like this stool, it moves. If two objects are exactly the same, the object that receives a bigger force will **accelerate**, or increase its speed," Clara said, pushing two stools at the same time.

"Which stool received a bigger force?" Clara asked.

"The one on the right. It went farther," said Liam.

"So, giving our car a big push at the top of the hill will cause it to accelerate and go faster," Alex summarized.

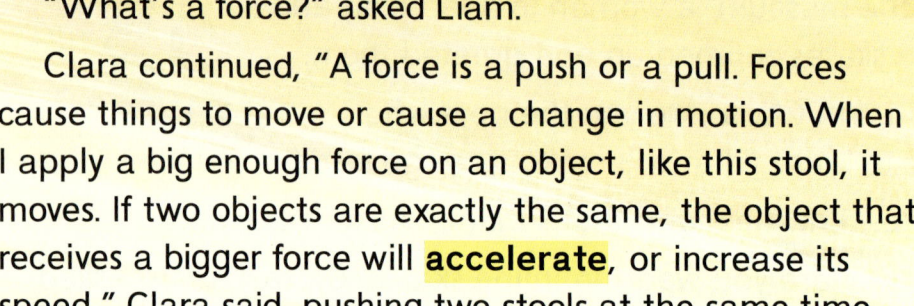

There's a sharp curve coming up!

I'm going to accelerate now!

GRAVITY AND FRICTION

Clara smiled, "Right! Another force acting on your car is **gravity**. Gravity is a pulling force between two objects." Clara took a tennis ball out of her pocket. "When I drop this ball, gravity pulls it towards the floor. It's the same force that pulls your car down the hill."

"So, a big push gives us an **advantage** over other cars, and gravity will keep us going. How do we stop?" Liam asked.

"You'll need **friction**. Friction is a force between two surfaces that slows objects down or stops them from moving. For example, I lean back on my skates, and the friction between the rubber stoppers and the floor slows me down," said Clara.

You need friction.

"Thanks, Clara! The virtual race car was cool! I knew we had the skills and **capabilities** to win the race, but now we have science on our side, too," Liam grinned.

? Make Connections

Talk about ways that science can help you understand how objects move.

How can science help you understand your favorite activities? **TEXT TO SELF**

Craig Phillips

Reread

When you read an informational text, you often come across information that is new to you. As you read "The Big Race," reread key sections of text to make sure you understand them and remember the information they contain.

 ## Find Text Evidence

As you read "The Big Race," the concept of acceleration may be new to you. Reread the "Forces at Work" section on page 38 to help you remember what *accelerate* means.

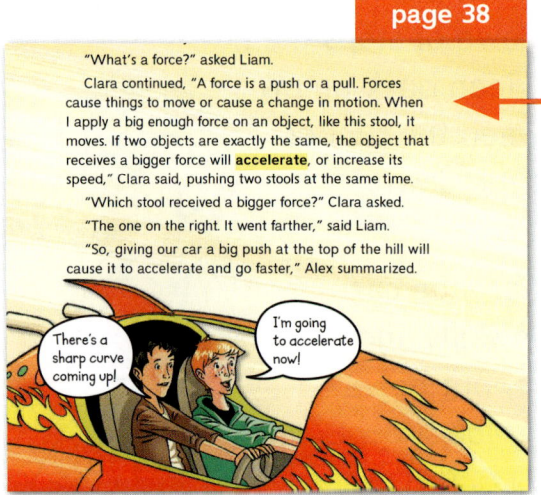

page 38

"What's a force?" asked Liam.

Clara continued, "A force is a push or a pull. Forces cause things to move or cause a change in motion. When I apply a big enough force on an object, like this stool, it moves. If two objects are exactly the same, the object that receives a bigger force will **accelerate**, or increase its speed," Clara said, pushing two stools at the same time.

"Which stool received a bigger force?" Clara asked.

"The one on the right. It went farther," said Liam.

"So, giving our car a big push at the top of the hill will cause it to accelerate and go faster," Alex summarized.

There's a sharp curve coming up!

I'm going to accelerate now!

I read that accelerate *means to increase the speed of something. Rereading will help me to understand and remember this concept.*

COLLABORATE

Your Turn

What does gravity do? Reread the "Gravity and Friction" section of "The Big Race" to find out. As you read, remember to use the strategy Reread.

Cause and Effect

Text structure is the way that authors organize information in a selection. Cause and effect is one kind of text structure. The author explains how and why something happens. A cause is why something happens. An effect is what happens.

 Find Text Evidence

I can reread "Forces at Work" in "The Big Race" on page 38 to find actions that cause something to happen. Then I can figure out the effects of those actions.

Cause	→	Effect
Clara applies force to one stool.	→	The stool moves.
Clara pushes both stools.	→	Both stools move.
Clara applies more force to one of the stools.	→	One stool moves farther.

COLLABORATE

Your Turn

Reread each section of "The Big Race." Find events or actions that cause something to happen and their effects. List each cause and effect in the graphic organizer.

Go Digital!
Use the interactive graphic organizer

41

Narrative Nonfiction

The selection "The Big Race" is narrative nonfiction.

Narrative nonfiction:
- Tells a story.
- Includes facts and examples about a topic.
- Often includes text features.

 ## Find Text Evidence

Even though "The Big Race" reads like a story, I can tell that it is an informational text because it includes facts and text features.

page 38

FORCES AT WORK

Alex and Liam climbed into the machine. Each seat had a steering wheel and a screen in front of it.

Clara said, "Since you want to build a fast car, you need to know about forces and how they affect motion."

"What's a force?" asked Liam.

Clara continued, "A force is a push or a pull. Forces cause things to move or cause a change in motion. When I apply a big enough force on an object, like this stool, it moves. If two objects are exactly the same, the object that receives a bigger force will **accelerate**, or increase its speed," Clara said, pushing two stools at the same time.

"Which stool received a bigger force?" Clara asked.

"The one on the right. It went farther," said Liam.

"So, giving our car a big push at the top of the hill will cause it to accelerate and go faster," Alex summarized.

A force is a push or pull.

There's a sharp curve coming up!

I'm going to accelerate now!

38

Text Features

Headings Headings tell what a section of text is mostly about.

Speech Balloons Speech Balloons tell what the characters are saying or thinking.

 COLLABORATE

Your Turn

Find two examples of text features in "The Big Race." Tell your partner what information you learned from the features.

Context Clues

When you are not sure what a word means, you can look at the other words around it to figure out the meaning. These other words, called context clues, may be **definitions, examples**, or **restatements** of the word's meaning.

 Find Text Evidence

When I read the fourth paragraph on page 38 of "The Big Race," I am not sure what the word force means. The phrase "a push or a pull" defines what the word force means.

Clara continued, "A force is a push or a pull. Forces cause things to move or cause a change in motion."

Your Turn

COLLABORATE

Use context clues to figure out the meanings of the following words in "The Big Race":

speed, *page 37*
friction, *page 39*
surfaces, *page 39*

Craig Phillips

Pages 36–39

Write About the Text

Henry

I answered the question: *What is the author's purpose for writing "The Big Race"? Use text evidence.*

Student Model: *Informative Text*

In "The Big Race," the author's purpose is to explain what will make a car go fast. Alex and Liam want to build a car for the soap box derby. Before they build it, they decide to visit the science museum for help.

Author's Purpose
My first sentence states the author's purpose for writing "The Big Race."

Sequence
I organized my writing in logical order by using linking words such as *before*.

While the boys are driving in a virtual race car, a scientist explains the different forces that affect motion. By the end, the boys know how to build their race car, and the reader understands how forces affect motion.

Grammar

This is an example of a **complex sentence**.

Grammar Handbook
See page 453.

Strong Conclusion
My final sentence sums up the author's purpose.

Your Turn

How does the author explain the concepts of *force* and *gravity* in "The Big Race"?

Go Digital!
Write your response online.
Use your editing checklist.

Creative Thinking

People come up with creative and original ideas every day. Sometimes a clever idea is the result of an accident, brainstorming, or observation.

► What do you think gave the boy in this photo the idea to build a motorcycle?

► What are some examples of clever ideas?

► Where do you get your ideas from?

Talk About It   COLLABORATE

Write words that describe how people think up ideas. Then talk to a partner about what helps you come up with good ideas.

Ideas

47

Vocabulary

Use the picture and the sentences to talk with a partner about each word.

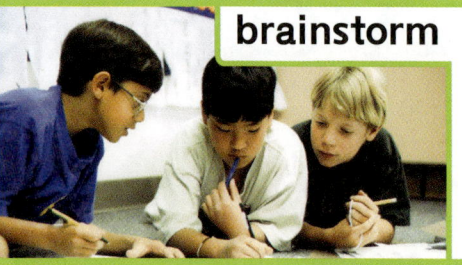

brainstorm

The boys began to **brainstorm** ideas for their project.

Describe a time you had to brainstorm some ideas.

flattened

Jess enjoyed rolling out the **flattened** dough.

What is something else that can be flattened?

frantically

The dog was **frantically** digging up sand.

Describe a time when you frantically searched for something.

gracious

Justin's mom is **gracious** and kind when his friend comes over.

What is an antonym for gracious?

muttered

Dan **muttered** to himself as he read my paper.

When might you mutter something instead of saying it loudly?

official

Signing the contract will make the sale **official**.

What is an example of an official document?

original

Maria's artwork was unique and **original**.

What do you think makes something original?

stale

Grandfather and Mia threw the hard, **stale** bread out for the birds to eat.

What other kinds of food get stale?

Your Turn

COLLABORATE

Pick three words. Write three questions for your partner to answer.

Go Digital! *Use the online visual glossary*

The Dragon Problem

? **Inquiry Question**

How do characters make decisions?

50

Once upon a time, long before computers, baseball, or pizza, there lived a young man named Liang. During the day, Liang helped his father build furniture. At night, he made unique, **original** toys for the children in the village. He made birds with flapping wings. He carved dragons with rippling, moving scales, sharp claws, and red eyes. Every child in the village had one of Liang's dragons.

Liang knew a lot about dragons because one lived nearby on a mountain. A few times a year, the dragon would swoop down on the village. He ate water buffalo, pigs, and any people unlucky enough to be around. The Emperor had done nothing to get rid of the dragon even though his summer palace was near Liang's village.

One day in May, the Emperor and his family arrived to take up residence at his summer palace. As the procession passed through the village, the **gracious** Princess Peng smiled kindly at Liang. He fell instantly in love.

At dinner that night, Liang told his father that he wanted to marry Princess Peng. His father almost choked on the **stale**, hard rice ball he was eating.

"You're joking," his father said when he finally could speak.

"I'm serious!" insisted Liang.

His father began laughing so hard that the old chair he was sitting on broke. He lay on top of the **flattened** chair still laughing.

Valerie Sokolova

"I'll show him," Liang **muttered** angrily as he stomped out of the room.

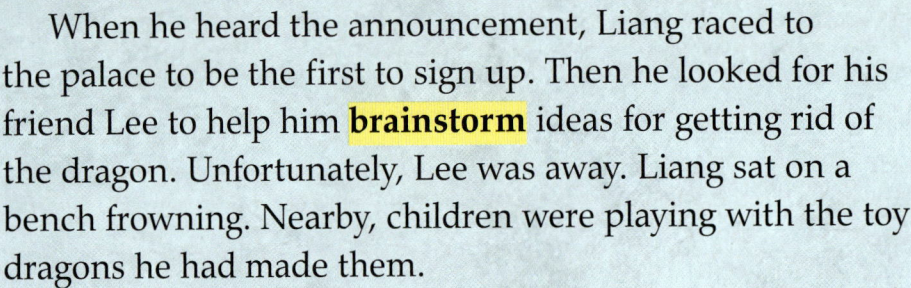

The next morning, the Emperor's messenger made an **official** announcement.

"His Most Noble Emperor proclaims that whoever gets rid of the dragon will marry his daughter, Princess Peng."

When he heard the announcement, Liang raced to the palace to be the first to sign up. Then he looked for his friend Lee to help him **brainstorm** ideas for getting rid of the dragon. Unfortunately, Lee was away. Liang sat on a bench frowning. Nearby, children were playing with the toy dragons he had made them.

"Liang, what's wrong?" the children asked.

"I have to get rid of the dragon on the mountain," he told them.

"I have an idea," said little Ling Ling. "Why don't you carve a giant dragon and leave it by the cave? It will alarm the real dragon and scare him into flying away."

Liang stared at her. "Perfect!" he shouted and rushed home. He worked **frantically** for days making a huge, scary dragon's head. The night he finished, he loaded it onto a cart and went up the mountain. When he got near the cave, Liang put the wooden head on top of a big rock. From the front, it looked like the rest of the dragon's body was behind the rock.

Liang hid in the bushes and gave a loud roar. "What's that noise?" growled the dragon rushing out of his cave. Then he saw the massive dragon head glaring at him. "Go away, or I'll eat you up," he commanded.

The huge dragon continued to glare at him. "He must be very strong. He's not afraid of me," thought the dragon, who, like all bullies, was a coward. He decided that now was a good time to take a long trip.

"Actually, I'm leaving now. Please make yourself at home in my cave," the dragon called out as he flew away.

A year later, Liang and Princess Peng were married. They opened a toy shop together and lived happily ever after.

Make Connections

? Talk about where Liang's idea for scaring the dragon came from.

Tell about a time when a friend helped you think of a good idea. TEXT TO SELF

Make Predictions

When you read the story "The Dragon Problem," you can use text clues and illustrations to predict what will happen next.

 ## Find Text Evidence

As I read, I see that Liang wants to marry Princess Peng. Then the Emperor announces that anyone who gets rid of the dragon will marry his daughter. My prediction that Liang will try to get rid of the dragon was correct.

page 52

"I'll show him," Liang **muttered** angrily as he stomped out of the room.

The next morning, the Emperor's messenger made an **official** announcement.

"His Most Noble Emperor proclaims that whoever gets rid of the dragon will marry his daughter, Princess Peng."

When he heard the announcement, Liang raced to the palace to be the first to sign up. Then he looked for his friend Lee to help him **brainstorm** ideas for getting rid of the dragon. Unfortunately, Lee was away. Liang sat on a bench frowning. Nearby, children were playing with the toy dragons he had made them.

"Liang, what's wrong?" the children asked.

I read that Liang is going to the palace to sign up to get rid of the dragon. My prediction was correct.

COLLABORATE

Your Turn

Make a prediction about whether the dragon will ever return to his cave. Tell what clues in the text led to your prediction. As you read, remember to use the strategy Make Predictions.

Sequence

Sequence is the order in which the key **story events** take place. Putting a story's events in sequence will help you to understand the **setting,** the **characters,** and the **plot.**

 ## Find Text Evidence

When I reread pages 51 and 52 of "The Dragon Problem," I see that Liang wants to marry Princess Peng. The next day, the Emperor's messenger announces that anyone who gets rid of the dragon will marry the princess.

Character   Liang
Setting   village in ancient China
Beginning   Liang sees Princess Peng and falls in love. The next day, the Emperor says anyone who gets rid of the dragon will marry the princess.
Middle
End

> Put key story events in order to help you summarize the plot.

Your Turn

COLLABORATE

Reread "The Dragon Problem." Find the important events in the middle and end of the story. List them in the graphic organizer.

Go Digital!
Use the interactive graphic organizer

Fairy Tale

"The Dragon Problem" is a fairy tale.

Fairy tales:

- Have a main character who must complete a difficult task or journey.
- Usually contain imaginary creatures.
- Include illustrations and have a happy ending.

 Find Text Evidence

"The Dragon Problem" is a fairy tale. The story's main character must complete a difficult task. The story includes an imaginary creature, a dragon.

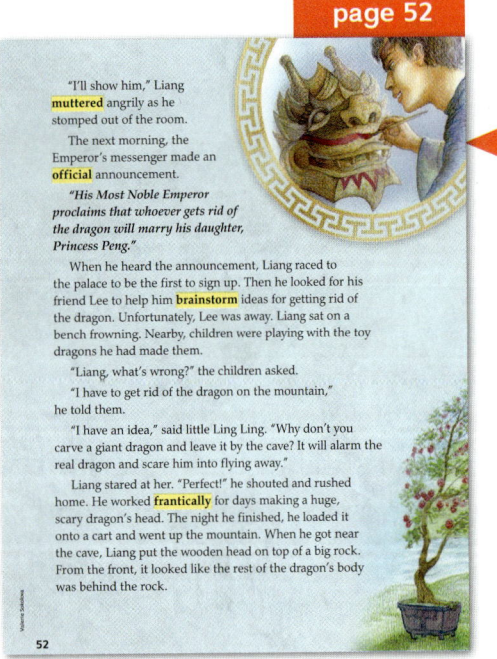

page 52

"I'll show him," Liang **muttered** angrily as he stomped out of the room.

The next morning, the Emperor's messenger made an **official** announcement.

"His Most Noble Emperor proclaims that whoever gets rid of the dragon will marry his daughter, Princess Peng."

When he heard the announcement, Liang raced to the palace to be the first to sign up. Then he looked for his friend Lee to help him **brainstorm** ideas for getting rid of the dragon. Unfortunately, Lee was away. Liang sat on a bench frowning. Nearby, children were playing with the toy dragons he had made them.

"Liang, what's wrong?" the children asked.

"I have to get rid of the dragon on the mountain," he told them.

"I have an idea," said little Ling Ling. "Why don't you carve a giant dragon and leave it by the cave? It will alarm the real dragon and scare him into flying away."

Liang stared at her. "Perfect!" he shouted and rushed home. He worked **frantically** for days making a huge, scary dragon's head. The night he finished, he loaded it onto a cart and went up the mountain. When he got near the cave, Liang put the wooden head on top of a big rock. From the front, it looked like the rest of the dragon's body was behind the rock.

52

Use Illustrations Fairy tales are usually illustrated. Illustrations give visual clues about the characters, settings, and events in the story.

COLLABORATE

Your Turn

With a partner, discuss whether the ending is surprising for a fairy tale. Explain why or why not.

Synonyms

As you read "The Dragon Problem," you may come across a word that you don't know. Look at the surrounding words and sentences for clues. Sometimes the author uses a synonym, a word that means almost the same thing as the unfamiliar word.

 Find Text Evidence

When I read the third sentence on page 51 in "The Dragon Problem," the word original *helps me to figure out what the word* unique *means.*

At night, he made unique, original toys for the children in the village.

 **Your Turn**

Look for synonyms to find the meanings of the following words in "The Dragon Problem."

rippling, *page 51*

alarm, *page 52*

massive, *page 53*

Valerie Sokolova

57

Write About the Text

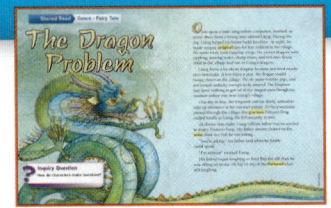

Pages 50–53

Kyle

I responded to the prompt: *Add an event to the story. Describe Liang's return to the village after scaring off the dragon. Use details from the story.*

Student Model: *Narrative Text*

Liang could not believe his luck.

The dragon was really gone! As proof,

he gathered a few of the glittering

scales that the dragon had left

behind. Then he raced back to

the village.

The children rushed to meet him. "Did

the plan really work?" Ling Ling asked.

Grammar

This is an example of an exclamatory **sentence**.

Grammar Handbook
See page 450.

Descriptive Details

I used sensory language to help readers visualize the story's events.

"The dragon flew away!" Liang said. He showed her the gleaming scales. Then the children marched with Liang to the Emperor's summer palace to share the good news. Liang couldn't wait to meet the princess!

Dialogue
I developed the characters' experiences with conversation.

Sequence
I used time-order words to tell the events as they happened.

Your Turn

Add an event to the story. Describe what happens when Liang tells his father he is marrying the princess. Use details from the story.

Go Digital!
Write your response online.
Use your editing checklist.

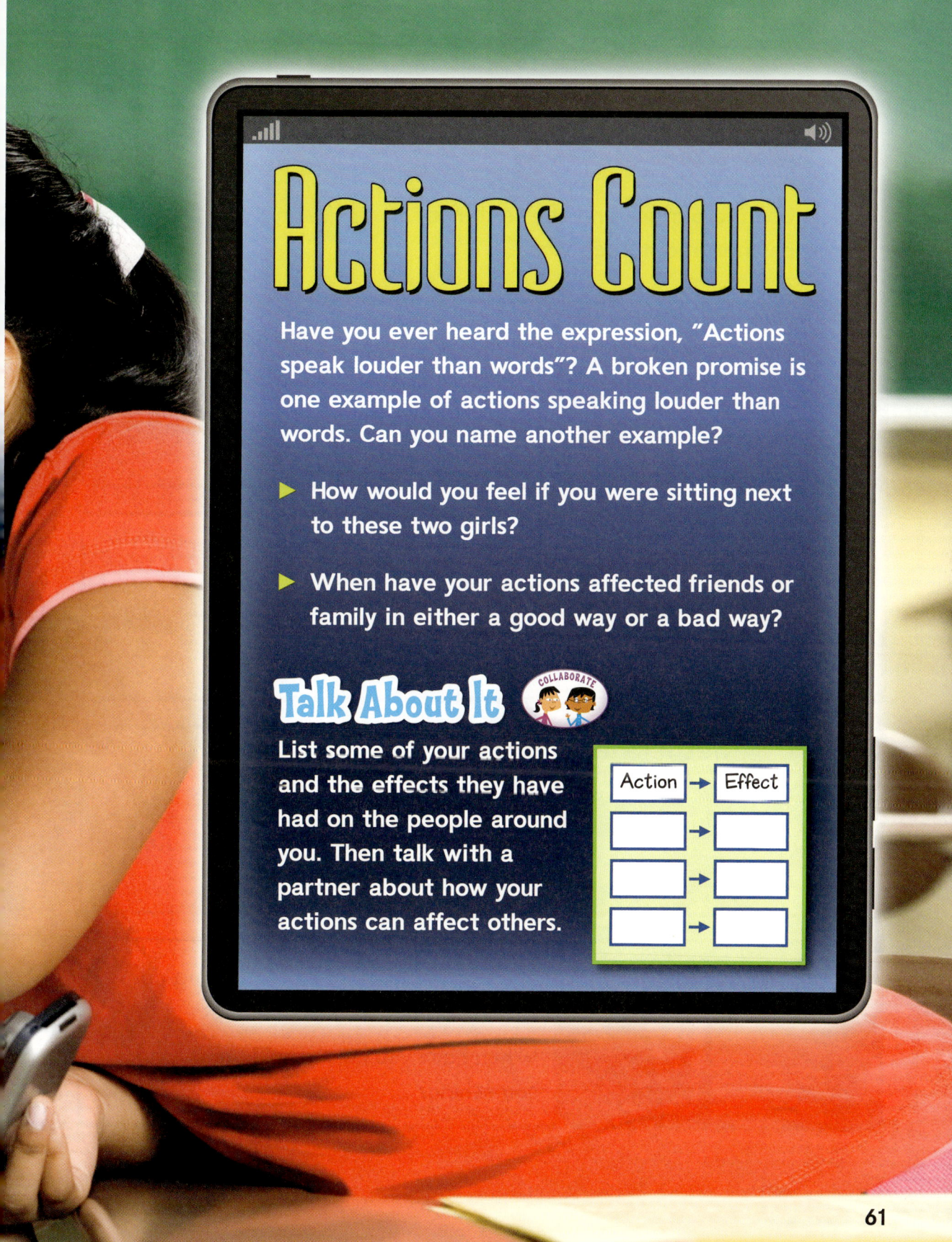

Actions Count

Have you ever heard the expression, "Actions speak louder than words"? A broken promise is one example of actions speaking louder than words. Can you name another example?

▶ How would you feel if you were sitting next to these two girls?

▶ When have your actions affected friends or family in either a good way or a bad way?

Talk About It

COLLABORATE

List some of your actions and the effects they have had on the people around you. Then talk with a partner about how your actions can affect others.

Action →	Effect
→	
→	
→	

Vocabulary

Use the picture and the sentences to talk with a partner about each word.

accountable

Sam is held **accountable** for washing his dog.

How are the words accountable and responsible similar?

advise

A coach can **advise** you on how to improve your swimming.

What is a synonym for advise?

desperately

The woman was **desperately** trying to remember where she had left her keys.

Describe a time when you desperately tried to remember something.

hesitated

The dog **hesitated** before jumping up to grab the food off the counter.

When have you hesitated before doing something?

humiliated

Sarah felt **humiliated** when she forgot her lines.

How is humiliated similar to embarrassed?

inspiration

The girl found **inspiration** for her drawing in nature.

When you have to write a story where does your inspiration come from?

self-esteem

Winning the soccer championship helped improve Billy's confidence and **self-esteem**.

What else builds self-esteem?

uncomfortably

Sonya's throat felt **uncomfortably** sore.

What are some things that can feel uncomfortably tight?

Your Turn

COLLABORATE

Pick three words. Write three questions for your partner to answer.

Go Digital! *Use the online visual glossary*

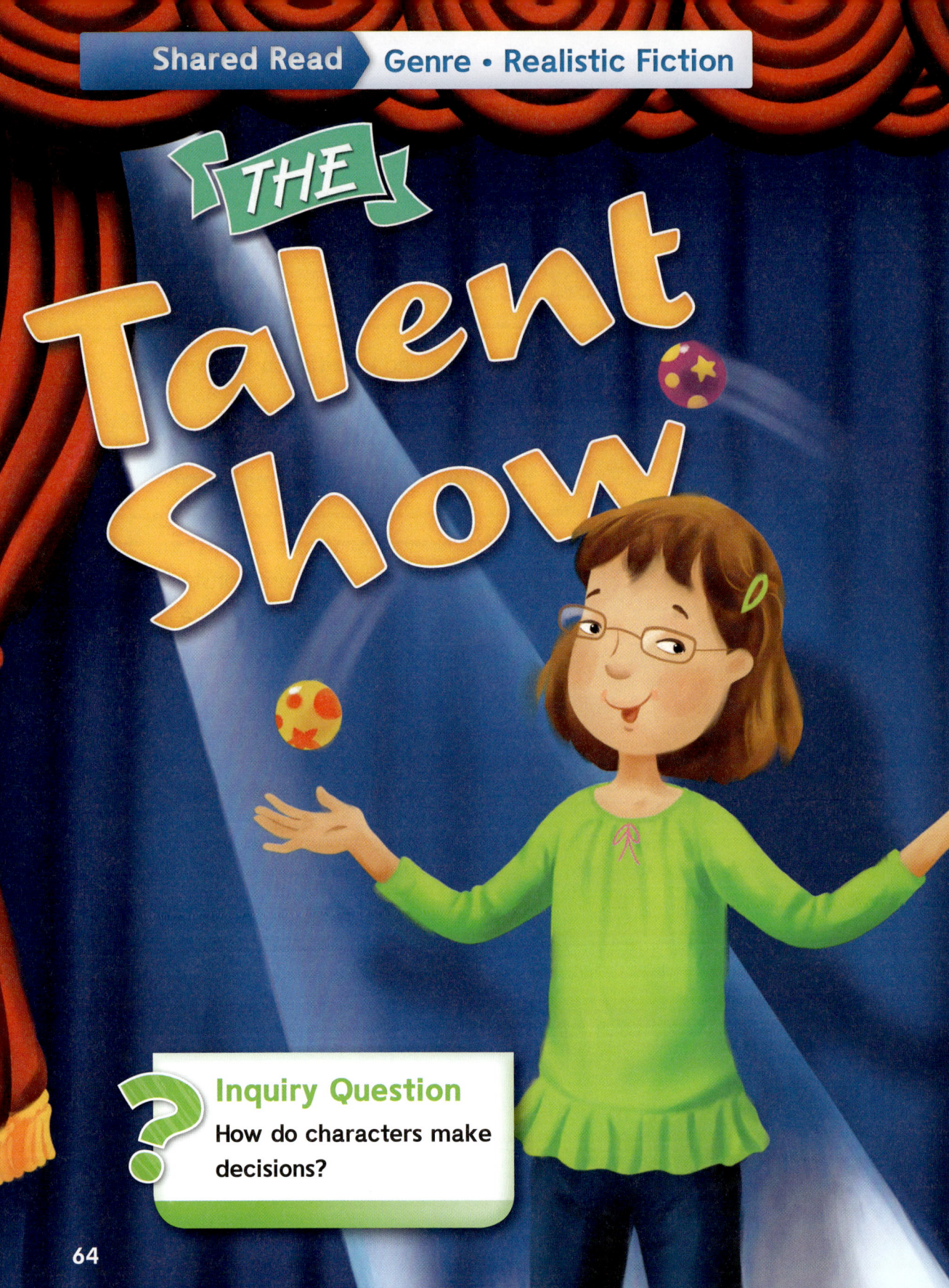

THE Talent Show

? **Inquiry Question**
How do characters make decisions?

"Tina, there's a school talent show in three weeks," I shouted to my best friend. My older brother had been teaching me juggling, and I knew he'd help me with my act for the show.

Tina ran over to the bulletin board and read the poster. "Maura, what's our act going to be?" Tina asked me.

"Our act?" I said, taking a tighter grip on my books.

Tina grinned, pointed to the poster and said "It says acts can be individuals, partners, or small groups."

My grip on my books became uncomfortably tight. "You want to do an act together?"

"It'll be fun," Tina said.

I hesitated for a second before continuing. "I've got an idea and. . . ."

Tina interrupted me. "Yeah, me too; let's talk at lunch."

During math, I tried to think of how I would tell Tina that I wanted to do my own act. After all, we are best friends; we should be able to see eye to eye about this. The problem is Tina always takes charge, I don't speak up, and then I end up feeling resentful about the whole situation.

I desperately wanted to win, but it was more than that. I wanted to win on my own—with an act that was all mine.

Chris Vallo

At lunch, Tina started talking as soon as we sat down. "I have it all planned out. My inspiration came from that new TV show, 'You've Got Talent.' We can sing along to a song and do a dance routine, and my mother can make us costumes."

"Yeah, that's good," I said. "But I had another idea." I told her about my juggling act.

Tina considered it. "Nah, I don't think I can learn to juggle in three weeks and I'd probably drop the balls," she said. "We don't want to be humiliated, right?"

At recess, I ran around the track a couple of times just to let off steam.

When my grandmother picked me up after school, she drove a few minutes and finally said, "Cat got your tongue?"

I explained about the talent show as she listened carefully. "So, Tina is not being respectful of your ideas, but it sounds as if you aren't either."

"What?" I shouted. "I told Tina her idea was good."

"No," said my grandmother, "I said that you weren't respectful of your *own* ideas, or you would have spoken up. I understand that you're friends, but you're still accountable for your own actions."

I thought about this. "So what should I do?" I asked.

"I **advise** you to tell the truth," she said. "It wouldn't hurt to let Tina know what you want. Besides," my grandmother added, "it will be good for your **self-esteem**!"

When we got home, I took 12 deep breaths, called Tina, and told her that I was going to do my juggling act. She was curt on the phone, and I spent all night worrying she would be mad at me.

The next day, she described her act and her costume. But the biggest surprise came at recess, when we played a game that I chose, not Tina.

I guess standing up for myself did pay off.

Make Connections

Talk about how Maura was affected by Tina's actions.

Tell about a time when someone wouldn't listen to your ideas. What did you do? TEXT TO SELF

Make Predictions

When you read, use story details to make predictions about what will happen. As you read "The Talent Show," make predictions.

 Find Text Evidence

You predicted that Tina is the kind of friend who is bossy. Reread page 65 of "The Talent Show" to find the text evidence that confirms your prediction.

page 65

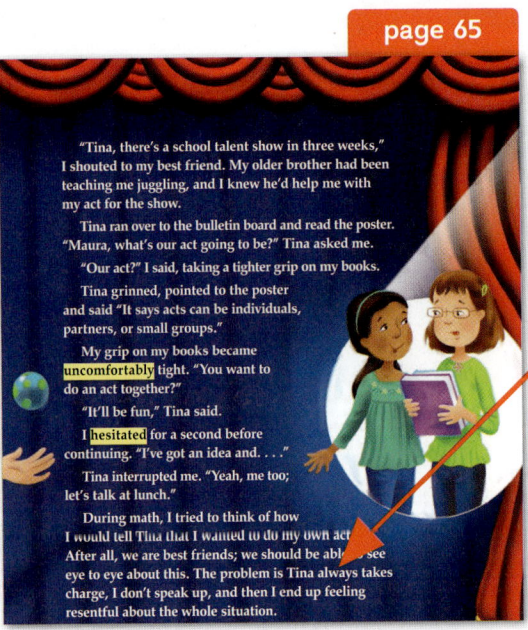

"Tina, there's a school talent show in three weeks," I shouted to my best friend. My older brother had been teaching me juggling, and I knew he'd help me with my act for the show.

Tina ran over to the bulletin board and read the poster. "Maura, what's our act going to be?" Tina asked me.

"Our act?" I said, taking a tighter grip on my books.

Tina grinned, pointed to the poster and said "It says acts can be individuals, partners, or small groups."

My grip on my books became uncomfortably tight. "You want to do an act together?"

"It'll be fun," Tina said.

I hesitated for a second before continuing. "I've got an idea and. . . ."

Tina interrupted me. "Yeah, me too; let's talk at lunch."

During math, I tried to think of how I would tell Tina that I wanted to do my own act. After all, we are best friends; we should be able to see eye to eye about this. The problem is Tina always takes charge, I don't speak up, and then I end up feeling resentful about the whole situation.

I read that Tina always takes charge. This confirms my prediction that Tina is bossy.

Your Turn

COLLABORATE

Using clues you find in the text, how do you predict Maura will solve a future problem? As you read, use the strategy Make Predictions.

Problem and Solution

The main **character** in a story usually has a problem that needs to be solved. The steps the character takes to solve the problem make up the **story's events**, the plot of the story.

 ## Find Text Evidence

As I reread pages 65 and 66 of "The Talent Show," I can see that Maura has a problem. I will list the events in the story. Then I can figure out how Maura finds a solution.

Character
Maura
Setting
Maura's school
Problem
Maura does not want to do an act with Tina.
Event
Tina tells Maura that they will do a dance act together.
Event
Solution

Your Turn

COLLABORATE

Reread "The Talent Show." Find other important story events. Use these events to identify the solution.

Go Digital!
Use the interactive graphic organizer

Realistic Fiction

The selection "The Talent Show" is realistic fiction.

Realistic Fiction:

- Is a made-up story.
- Has characters, settings, and events that could exist in real life.
- Includes dialogue.

Find Text Evidence

I can tell that "The Talent Show" is realistic fiction. The story mostly takes place at school. On page 65, Maura and Tina act and speak like real people who might go to my school.

page 65

"Tina, there's a school talent show in three weeks," I shouted to my best friend. My older brother had been teaching me juggling, and I knew he'd help me with my act for the show.

Tina ran over to the bulletin board and read the poster. "Maura, what's our act going to be?" Tina asked me.

"Our act?" I said, taking a tighter grip on my books.

Tina grinned, pointed to the poster and said "It says acts can be individuals, partners, or small groups."

My grip on my books became uncomfortably tight. "You want to do an act together?"

"It'll be fun," Tina said.

I hesitated for a second before continuing. "I've got an idea and. . . ."

Tina interrupted me. "Yeah, me too; let's talk at lunch."

During math, I tried to think of how I would tell Tina that I wanted to do my own act. After all, we are best friends; we should be able to see eye to eye about this. The problem is Tina always takes charge, I don't speak up, and then I end up feeling resentful about the whole situation.

I desperately wanted to win, but it was more than that. I wanted to win on my own—with an act that was all mine.

65

Dialogue Dialogue is the exact words the characters say.

Your Turn

COLLABORATE

With a partner, list two examples from "The Talent Show" that let you know it is realistic fiction.

Idioms

Idioms are phrases that have a meaning different from the meaning of each word in them. Sometimes context clues can help you figure out the meaning of an idiom.

 Find Text Evidence

When I read the idiom see eye to eye *on page 65 in "The Talent Show," the words* After all, we are best friends *help me figure out its meaning. To* see eye to eye *means to agree.*

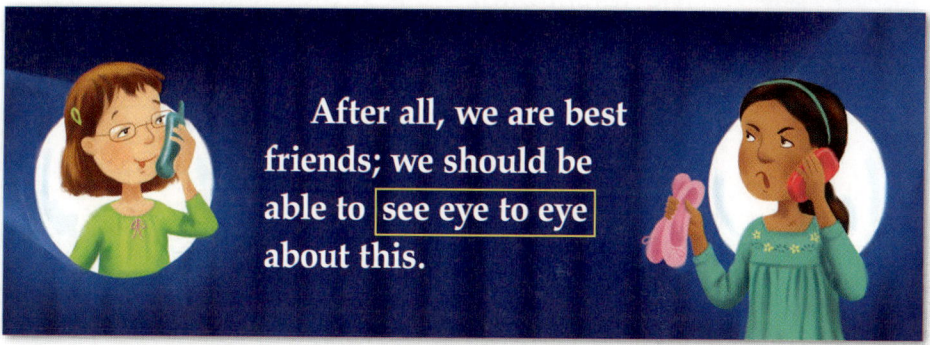

After all, we are best friends; we should be able to see eye to eye about this.

Your Turn

COLLABORATE

Use context clues to help you understand the meanings of the following idioms in "The Talent Show":

let off steam, *page 66*

cat got your tongue, *page 66*

standing up for myself, *page 67*

List some other idioms and their meanings.

Write About the Text

Pages 64–67

Petra

I responded to the prompt: *Write a dialogue of the phone conversation between Maura and Tina. Include details from the story.*

Student Model: *Narrative Text*

"Hey, Tina. It's Maura. We need to talk about the talent show."

"Sure!" Tina replied. "I've got our song picked out, and Mom is going to make us cool purple costumes. I picked out the material for them. Can you come over and practice?"

Focus on an Event
I wrote a realistic phone conversation between Tina and Maura.

Dialogue
I used informal language to show the characters' responses to situations.

"Um, actually, I need to tell you something, Tina. I'm going to do my own act," I said nervously. I paused and gulped. "I'm going to juggle."

"Oh, you want to do your own act. I see," Tina said. "Okay. See you at school tomorrow."

Grammar

Complete sentences have a **subject** and a **predicate**.

Grammar Handbook See page 451.

Precise Words
The strong verbs I used help describe how Maura felt.

Your Turn

Write a dialogue between Maura and Tina in which Maura chooses the game at recess. Use details from the story.

Go Digital!
Write your response online.
Use your editing checklist.

73

74

RISE
TO THE CHALLENGE

How do you start a business and help people at the same time? A woman in New York did it. She started a bakery that includes a culinary training program for immigrants. Not only has the training program been successful, the bakery's breads are a big hit too.

▶ How do you think a business can give back to the community? What kinds of things could they do?

▶ What kind of business would you start? How would it help people or your community?

Talk About It

Write words that tell how starting a business can help people. Then talk about a business you would like to start.

Starting a Business

Vocabulary

Use the picture and the sentences to talk with a partner about each word.

compassionate

I could tell she was a **compassionate** and caring person by the way she hugged her sister.

What is an antonym for compassionate?

enterprise

Starting a white water rafting business was an exciting new **enterprise** for Tom.

What is the first thing a person starting a new enterprise might do?

exceptional

Monica is an **exceptional** and talented flute player.

How does a person become exceptional at doing something?

funds

Nicole's class held a bake sale to raise **funds** to buy books for the library.

What project would you like to raise funds for?

innovative

Sam enjoyed trying out the new **innovative** racing wheelchair.

What new technology do you think is innovative?

process

An important step in the **process** of making a pie is to roll out the crust.

What is one step in the process of baking cookies?

routine

Brittany loved the daily **routine** of walking her dog.

Why is it helpful to have a morning routine?

undertaking

Cleaning up Tim's messy bedroom was going to be a big **undertaking**.

What would you consider a big undertaking?

COLLABORATE

Your Turn

Pick three words. Write three questions for your partner to answer.

Go Digital! *Use the online visual glossary*

Inquiry Question

How does the author choose a particular genre for a story?

Dollars and $ENSE

Behind the success of these big businesses is a desire to help others.

Good business is not always about the bottom line. A **compassionate** company knows that making money is not the only way to measure success. Many large businesses in the United States and all over the world are finding unusual ways to help people in need.

Hearts and Soles

After starting and running four businesses, Blake Mycoskie wanted a break from his usual **routine**. In 2006, he traveled to Argentina, in South America, and while he was there he learned to sail and dance. He also visited poor villages where very few of the children had shoes. Mycoskie decided he had to do something. "I'm going to start a shoe company, and for every pair I sell, I'm going to give one pair to a kid in need."

For this new **undertaking**, Mycoskie started the business using his own money. He named it TOMS: Shoes for Tomorrow. The slip-on shoes are modeled on shoes that are traditionally worn by Argentine workers.

Mycoskie immediately set up his **innovative** one-for-one program. TOMS gives away one pair of shoes for every pair that is purchased. Later that year, Mycoskie returned to Argentina and gave away 10,000 pairs of shoes. By 2011, TOMS had donated over one million pairs.

TOMS' employees unpack shoes to give away.

The company has expanded to sell eyeglasses. In a similar program, one pair of eyeglasses is donated for every pair that is bought.

Mycoskie is pleased and surprised. "I always thought I would spend the first half of my life making money and the second half giving it away," Mycoskie says. "I never thought I could do both at the same time."

Giving Back Rocks!

Have you ever seen a Hard Rock Cafe? The company runs restaurants and hotels. In 1990, the company launched a new **enterprise**: charity. Since then, it has given away millions of dollars to different causes. Its motto is Love All, Serve All.

One way the company raises **funds** for charity is by selling a line of T-shirts. The **process** starts with rock stars designing the art that goes on the shirts. Then the shirts are sold on the Internet. Part of the money that is raised from the sales of the shirts is given to charity.

Employees at Hard Rock Cafe locations are encouraged to raise money for their community. Every store does it differently.

The Hard Rock Cafes are successful and give back to the community.

Top Five Biggest Charities

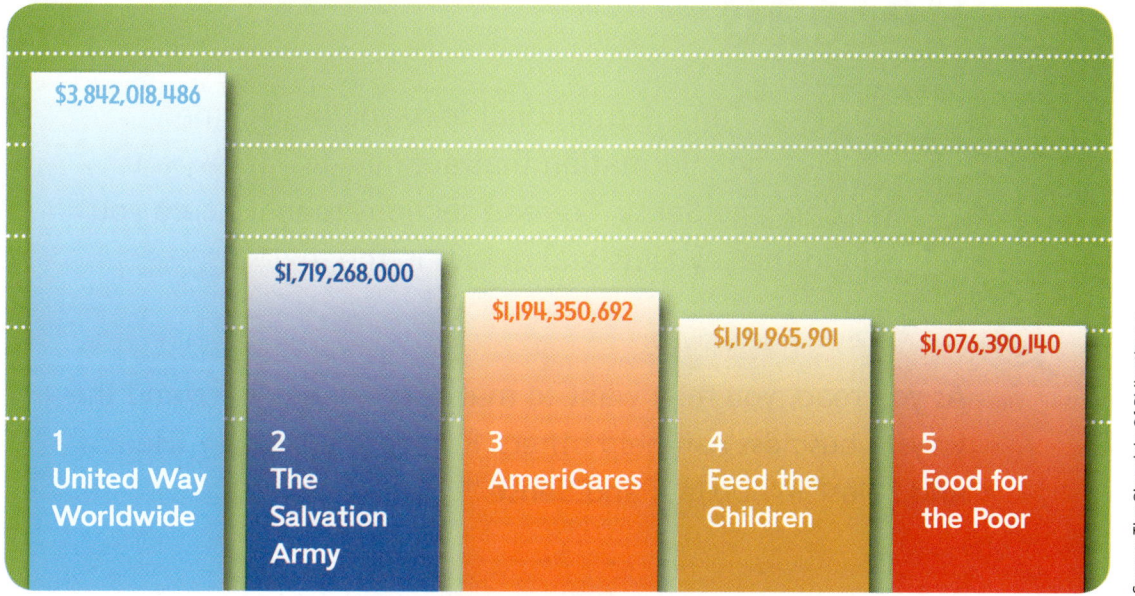

$3,842,018,486

$1,719,268,000

$1,194,350,692

$1,191,965,901

$1,076,390,140

1
United Way
Worldwide

2
The
Salvation
Army

3
AmeriCares

4
Feed the
Children

5
Food for
the Poor

Source: The Chronicle Of Philanthropy

Individuals as well as businesses are committed to helping people in need. This graph shows the American charities that got the most donations in one recent year and how much money they raised.

The restaurant in Hollywood, Florida, worked with some **exceptional** students from two Florida high schools. Together, they put on an event to raise money for the Make-A-Wish Foundation. The foundation grants wishes to children with serious medical problems.

The Bottom Line

Every day companies are thinking of innovative ways to give back to their community. If you own a business, making a profit is important. However, helping others is just as important as the bottom line. Helping others is good business!

Make Connections

How do the two companies profiled in this article help others?

If you owned a business, how would you use some of your profits to help others? **TEXT TO SELF**

Reread

When you read an informational text, you may come across ideas and information that are new to you. As you read "Dollars and Sense," reread sections to make sure you understand the key facts and details in the text.

 ## Find Text Evidence

As you read, you may want to make sure you understand the ways a business can help others. Reread the section "Hearts and Soles" in "Dollars and Sense."

page 79

Good business is not always about the bottom line. A **compassionate** company knows that making money is not the only way to measure success. Many large businesses in the United States and all over the world are finding unusual ways to help people in need.

Hearts and Soles

After starting and running four businesses, Blake Mycoskie wanted a break from his usual **routine**. In 2006, he traveled to Argentina, in South America, and while he was there he learned to sail and dance. He also visited poor villages where very few of the children had shoes. Mycoskie decided he had to do something. "I'm going to start a shoe company, and for every pair I sell, I'm going to give one pair to a kid in need."

For this new **undertaking**, Mycoskie started the business using his own money. He named it TOMS: Shoes for Tomorrow. The slip-on shoes are modeled on shoes that are traditionally worn by Argentine workers.

Mycoskie immediately set up his **innovative** one-for-one program. TOMS gives away one pair of shoes for every pair that is purchased. Later that year, Mycoskie returned to Argentina and gave away 10,000 pairs of shoes. By 2011, TOMS had donated over one million pairs.

I read that TOMS gives one pair of shoes for every pair of shoes someone buys. From this text evidence, I can draw the inference that the more shoes TOMS sells, the more shoes can be given away.

Your Turn

What is another example of a company giving back to the community? Reread page 80 to answer the question. As you read other selections, remember to use the strategy Reread.

Main Idea and Key Details

The main idea is the most important idea that an author presents in a text or a section of text. Key details give important information to support the main idea.

 ## Find Text Evidence

When I reread the second paragraph in the section "Giving Back Rocks!" on page 80 of "Dollars and Sense," I can identify the key details. Next I can think about what the details have in common. Then I can figure out the main idea of the section.

Main Idea

Hard Rock Cafe sells a line of T-shirts to raise funds for charity.

> Key details tell about the main idea.

Detail

Rock stars design the art that goes on the shirts.

Detail

The shirts are sold on the Internet.

Detail

Part of the money that is raised from the sales of the shirts is given to charity.

Your Turn   COLLABORATE

Reread the section "Hearts and Soles" on pages 79–80 of "Dollars and Sense." Find the key details in the section and list them in your graphic organizer. Use the details to determine the main idea.

Go Digital!
Use the interactive graphic organizer

Persuasive Article

"Dollars and Sense" is a persuasive article.

A persuasive article:

- Is nonfiction.
- States the writer's opinion on a topic.
- Provides facts and examples.
- May include text features such as headings and graphs.

 ### Find Text Evidence

"Dollars and Sense" is a persuasive article. It states the author's opinion and tries to get readers to agree. It includes headings and a graph that shows the amount of money raised by different charities.

page 81

TIME
FOR KIDS

Top Five Biggest Charities

$3,842,018,486 | $1,719,268,000 | $1,194,350,692 | $1,191,965,901 | $1,076,390,140

1 United Way Worldwide | 2 The Salvation Army | 3 AmeriCares | 4 Feed the Children | 5 Food for the Poor

Source: The Chronicle Of Philanthropy

Individuals as well as businesses are committed to helping people in need. This graph shows the American charities that got the most donations in one recent year and how much money they raised.

The restaurant in Hollywood, Florida, worked with some **exceptional** students from two Florida high schools. Together, they put on an event to raise money for the Make-A-Wish Foundation. The foundation grants wishes to children with serious medical problems.

The Bottom Line

Every day companies are thinking of innovative ways to give back to their community. If you own a business, making a profit is important. However, helping others is just as important as the bottom line. Helping others is good business!

Make Connections

How do the two companies profiled in this article help others?

If you owned a business, how would you use some of your profits to help others? TEXT TO SELF

81

Text Features

Graph Graphs help you picture numerical information. A bar graph helps you compare information.

Headings Headings tell you what the section is mostly about.

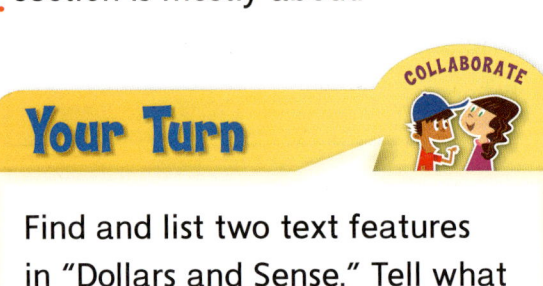

COLLABORATE

Your Turn

Find and list two text features in "Dollars and Sense." Tell what information you learned from each of the features.

Suffixes

A suffix is a word part added to the end of a word to change its meaning. Knowing some common suffixes can help you to figure out the meanings of unfamiliar words. Look at the suffixes below:

-ly = done in the way of

-ive = related or belonging to

-ful = full of or characterized by

 ## Find Text Evidence

I see the word innovative *on page 79 of "Dollars and Sense." Looking at its word parts, I see the root word* innovate. *The suffix* -ive *changes a word into an adjective. This will help me to figure out what* innovative *means.*

Mycoskie immediately set up his innovative one-for-one program. TOMS gives away one pair of shoes for every pair that is purchased.

 ## Your Turn

Use suffixes and context clues to figure out the meanings of the following words:

immediately, *page 79*

traditionally, *page 79*

successful, *page 80*

Ho/Toms Shoe/AP Images

Pages 78–81

Write About the Text

Kendall

I answered the question: *Do you agree with the author's opinion in "Dollars and Sense"? Include text evidence in your answer.*

Student Model: *Opinion*

> The author of "Dollars and Sense" believes that successful businesses don't just make money. They also help others. I agree with the author's opinion because I think it is important to help others. People support businesses, and businesses should help people in return.

Sentence Length

My sentences have different lengths to make my writing more interesting.

Grammar

Avoid **run-on sentences** by using linking words such as *because*.

Grammar Handbook

See page 454.

Stockbyte/Getty Images

For instance, Blake Mycoskie gives away one pair of shoes for every pair he sells. He shows that businesses can make money and help people at the same time. In this case, people are more willing to buy the brand because of the donation. When businesses help others, everyone wins.

Reasons and Evidence
I used facts and examples to support my opinion.

Strong Conclusion
My last line sums up my opinion.

Your Turn

Which company in "Dollars and Sense" is doing more to help people? Include text evidence in your answer.

Go Digital!
Write your response online.
Use your editing checklist.

Kwaku Alston/Stockland Martel

Contents

Adjectives

Adverbs

Negatives

Prepositions

Mechanics: Abbreviations

Mechanics: Capitalization

Mechanics: Punctuation

Sentences

Sentences and Sentence Fragments

A **sentence** expresses a complete thought. A **sentence fragment** does not express a complete thought.

Al writes about the storm. (complete sentence)
The heavy rains. (needs a predicate)

Your Turn Write each group of words. Write sentence or fragment next to it to identify each item. Then rewrite each fragment to make a complete sentence.

1. We listened to the news reports.
2. The strong winds.

Sentence Types

Each of the four types of sentences begins with a **capital letter** and ends with an **end mark**.

A **declarative sentence** makes a statement. It ends with a **period**.	*Scott rode a horse last week.*
An **interrogative sentence** asks a question. It ends with a **question mark**.	*Did you see him on the trail?*
A **imperative sentence** tells or asks someone to do something. It ends with a **period**.	*Take a picture of the group.*
An **exclamatory sentence** shows strong feeling. It ends with an **exclamation mark**.	*We had a great time riding!*

Your Turn Write each sentence. Add the correct punctuation. Then write what kind of sentence it is.

1. I had never been on a horse
2. Do you know how to ride a horse

Simple and Compound Sentences

A **simple sentence** has only one complete thought. A **compound sentence** has two or more complete thoughts. The **coordinating conjunctions** *and, but,* and *or* connect the complete thoughts in a compound sentence.

> *My mother works in the city.* (simple sentence)
> *My mother works in the city,* **but** *my father works at home.*
> *(compound sentence)*

Your Turn Write each sentence. Then tell whether the sentence is *simple* or *compound.* If it is a compound sentence, circle the coordinating conjunction.

1. My brother volunteers at the library.
2. He works on Saturdays, and Mom drives him there.
3. I would join him, but my team practices that day.
4. You can walk home, or Dad can pick you up.
5. Some days everyone is doing different things.

Complete Subjects and Complete Predicates

Every sentence has two important parts: the **subject** and the **predicate**.

The **subject** tells whom or what the sentence is about. The **complete subject** is all the words in the subject part.

> *The woman next door works in her garden.*

The **predicate** tells what the subject does or is. The **complete predicate** is all the words in the predicate.

> *The woman next door works in her garden.*

Your Turn Write each sentence. Underline the complete subject. Circle the complete predicate.

1. Our neighbor grows his own vegetables.
2. He plants three different gardens.
3. My sister and I help.
4. Will he invite us to dinner?
5. His recipe for tomato soup is the best!

Simple Subjects and Simple Predicates

The **simple subject** is the main word in the complete subject.

> Our *vacation* in Boston starts on Saturday.

The **simple predicate** is the main word in the complete predicate.

> Our vacation in Boston **starts** on Saturday.

Your Turn Write each sentence. Underline the simple subject. Circle the simple predicate.

1. The dog charged after the rabbit.
2. The dog's owner then chased after him.

Compound Subjects and Compound Predicates

A **compound subject** contains two or more simple subjects that have the same predicate.

> The **cat** and **dog** *ran outside.*

A **compound predicate** contains two more simple predicates that have the same subject.

> The cat **sat** and **meowed** *at the door.*

Use the **conjunction** *and* or *or* to combine sentences and create compound subjects or compound predicates. When you combine three or more simple subjects or simple predicates, use **commas** to separate them.

> Jan stepped outside. Jan turned left. Jan headed home.
> Jan stepped outside, turned left, and headed home.
> (compound predicate)

Your Turn Combine the sentence pairs to form one sentence. Then write whether the new sentence has a compound subject or a compound predicate.

1. Dad raked the yard. Mom raked the yard.
2. Mom mowed the lawn. Mom washed the car.

Complex Sentences

A **complex sentence** contains an independent clause and one or more dependent clauses.

We pitched our tent where the ground was flat and dry.

An **independent clause** can stand alone as a sentence.

We pitched our tent.

A **dependent clause** cannot stand alone as a sentence and begins with a **subordinating conjunction**. Some common subordinating conjunctions are *after, although, before, because, during, if, since, until, when, where,* and *while.*

where the ground was flat and dry

Use a **comma** after the dependent clause when it comes at the beginning of a sentence.

After the sun went down, we heard an owl.

Your Turn Write each sentence. Underline the independent clause. Circle the dependent clause.

1. We looked up at the sky after it got dark.
2. You might see a shooting star if you wait long enough.
3. While we were watching, the Moon rose above the trees.
4. When I grow up, I might become an astronaut.
5. We talked until our parents told us to go to sleep.

Run-On Sentences

A **run-on sentence** contains two or more independent clauses without the proper conjunctions or punctuation.

I dropped a book my cat got scared it ran away.

You can correct run-on sentences using one or more strategies.

Break the independent clauses into separate sentences.	*I dropped a book. My cat got scared. It ran away.*
Create a compound subject or compound predicate.	*I dropped a book. My cat got scared and ran away.*
Create a compound sentence using coordinating conjunctions.	*I dropped a book, and my cat got scared and ran away.*
Create a complex sentence using subordinating conjunctions.	*Because I dropped a book, my cat got scared and ran away.*

Your Turn **Correct each run-on sentence using one or more of the strategies described above.**

1. My alarm didn't go off I missed the bus.
2. Mom was already at work I had to walk.
3. The sun was out it was really chilly.
4. I got to school I raced up to the door.
5. I was so embarrassed it was closed it was Saturday!

Nouns

Singular and Plural Nouns

A **noun** names a person, place, thing, or idea. It can be a single word or a group of words used together. A **singular noun** names one person, place, thing, or idea. A **plural noun** names more than one. Add *-s* to form the plural of most nouns. Add *-es* to form the plural of nouns ending in *s, x, ch,* or *sh*.

Singular nouns: boy   school   home run   joy
Plural nouns: girls   stores   churches   beliefs

Your Turn Write each sentence. Underline each noun and write whether it is singular or plural.

1. The actor needed to learn his lines.
2. His friend read from the script.

More Plural Nouns

If a noun ends in a consonant + *y*, change *y* to *i* and add *-es*.	*ladies, berries, skies, libraries*
If a noun ends in a vowel + *y*, add *-s*.	*boys, monkeys, days, essays*
If a noun ends in *-f*, you may need to change *f* to *v* and add *-es*.	*chefs, roofs, leaves, hooves, knives*
Some nouns have the same singular and plural forms.	*deer, sheep, moose, fish*
Some nouns have special plural forms.	*men, women, children, teeth, feet*

Your Turn Write each sentence. Change the singular noun in parentheses ( ) into a plural noun.

1. The park is crowded on (holiday).
2. Many (child) visit with their parents.
3. If there are sunny (sky), they play outside.

Common and Proper Nouns

A **common noun** names any person, place, or thing. A **proper noun** names a particular person, place, or thing. A proper noun always begins with a capital letter.

> The **student** looked at the **map**. *(common)*
> **Brittany** located **Ohio**. *(proper)*

Your Turn Write each sentence. Underline each noun and write whether it is common or proper.

1. Anna has a map of the world on her wall.
2. There are pins placed in several countries.

Concrete and Abstract Nouns

A **concrete noun** names a person, place, or thing that physically exists and can be perceived with the senses. An **abstract noun** names a quality, concept, or idea that does not physically exist. Many abstract nouns have no plural form.

> **Ellen** set the **sheet music** on the **piano**. *(concrete)*
> **Music** fills the **soul** with **happiness**. *(abstract)*

Collective Nouns

A **collective noun** names a group acting as a single unit. Collective nouns can also have plural forms.

> Our **team** plays three other **teams** next week.

Your Turn Write each sentence. Underline each noun and write whether it is concrete or abstract. Circle any collective nouns.

1. The road crew stopped traffic on our street.
2. My sisters wanted to go to the shopping mall.
3. Their car was stopped for a long time.

Singular and Plural Possessive Nouns

A **possessive noun** is a noun that shows who or what owns or has something.

A singular possessive noun is formed by adding an **apostrophe (')** + s to the end of a singular noun.

The car's alarm made the boy's ears hurt.

Most plural nouns ending in -s become possessive by adding an apostrophe to the end. Irregular plural nouns that don't end in -s add an apostrophe + s.

The visitors' center hosted a children's reception.

Your Turn Write each sentence. Change the word in parentheses into a possessive noun.

1. My (brother) band practices in the garage.
2. The (group) poster shows their lead singers.
3. The two (singers) voices sound alike.
4. They played at our (school) fall festival.
5. All of the (newspapers) reviews were good.

Combining Sentences: Nouns

You can combine nouns in the subject.

Sean went inside. Cora went inside.
Sean and Cora went inside.

You can combine nouns in the predicate.

Mom likes checkers. Mom likes chess.
Mom likes checkers and chess.

Your Turn Combine the nouns in the sentence pairs to form one sentence.

1. Chet went to the shore. Emily went to the shore.
2. They saw sea gulls. They saw pelicans.
3. A boy swam nearby. An older woman swam nearby.
4. The snack bar sold juice. The snack bar sold fruit.
5. Were your friends there? Were your parents there?

Verbs

Action Verbs

An **action verb** is a word that expresses action. It tells what the subject does or did.

*The pitcher **threw** the ball over the plate.*

Your Turn Write each sentence. Underline the action verb(s).

1. Volunteers gathered in the city park.
2. They painted the information booth.
3. One crew repaired all the picnic tables.

Verb Tenses

A **present-tense verb** shows action that happens now.

*Today, the lifeguard **watches** the weather.*

A **past-tense verb** shows action that has already happened.

*Yesterday, the lifeguard **listened** for thunder.*

A **future-tense verb** shows action that may or will happen.

*At the first sign of lightning, he **will close** the pool.*

A **progressive tense** shows action that continues over time. Use the verb *be* with the *-ing* form of another verb to create the **present progressive, past progressive,** or **future progressive** tense.

*I **am watching** you. (present progressive)*

*I **was watching** you. (past progressive)*

*I **will be watching** you. (future progressive)*

Your Turn Write each sentence. Underline the verb and tell what tense it is.

1. Next summer I will attend space camp.
2. I received a brochure in the mail last week.
3. My mother helps me with the registration process.
4. I will be checking the camp's Web site every day now.
5. I am counting the days until the start of the program.

Subject-Verb Agreement

A present-tense verb must agree with the subject of the sentence. Add -s to most verbs if the subject is singular. Add -es to verbs that end in s, ch, sh, x, or z. Do not add -s or -es if the subject is plural or *I* or *you*.

Cristen **watches** the race. Her friends **cheer** for her sister.

Your Turn Write each sentence. Use the correct form of the verb(s) in parentheses.

1. The racers (crouch) at the starting line.
2. The clock (count) down the seconds.
3. Cristen's sister (rush) off to a great start.
4. She (take) the lead right away.
5. Another runner (catch) up and (challenge) her.

Spelling Present- and Past-Tense Verbs

The spelling of some verbs changes when -es or -ed is added. For verbs ending in a consonant + *y*, change the *y* to *i* before adding -es or -ed. For verbs ending in one vowel and one consonant, double the final consonant before adding -ed. For verbs ending in *e*, drop the *e* before adding -ed.

Josh **cried** when the music **stopped**. He truly **loved** that song.

Your Turn Write each sentence. Use the correct form of the verb in parentheses.

1. Now Josh (carry) his guitar upstairs.
2. He (try) to remember the song.
3. Yesterday he (practice) all day.
4. He (step) up to the challenge and worked hard.
5. Who (worry) that he may forget the words?

Main Verbs and Helping Verbs

The **main verb** in a sentence tells what the subject does or is. A **helping verb** helps the main verb show an action or make a statement. The verb *be* is often used as a helping verb.

> Carol *is running* for class president.

Use a **contraction** to combine a helping verb with the subject or with the word *not*. An **apostrophe (')** takes the place of the missing letters.

> *Carol's* feeling sad. Her friends *aren't* helping much.

Your Turn Write each sentence. Underline the main verbs and circle the helping verbs. If there is a contraction, tell which two words have been combined.

1. Many students are making posters.
2. Carol is preparing a speech.
3. Her school is holding a debate tomorrow.
4. Reporters were writing about it last week.
5. Carol's hoping that she will win the election.

Helping Verbs: *has, have, had*

The helping verbs *has, have,* and *had* can be used with the past-tense form of a verb to show an action that has already happened. When *has* or *have* is used, the entire verb forms the **present perfect tense**. When *had* is used, the entire verb forms the **past perfect tense**.

> She *has eaten* all of the bread he *had baked*.

Your Turn Write each sentence. Choose the correct form of *has, have,* or *had* to complete the sentence.

1. He (have, had) cooked every day last week.
2. Today she (has, had) watched him make dried fruit.
3. (Have, Has) you ever tasted anything so delicious?

Helping Verbs: *can, may, must*

The verbs *can, may,* and *must* can be used as **helping verbs** with a main verb.

*They **may wait** until someone **can help** them.*

Your Turn Write each sentence. Underline each main verb and circle each helping verb.

1. We may buy a gift for our parents.
2. What can we afford?
3. There must be something good here!
4. "Can I borrow some money?" I ask.
5. You reply, "We must stay within our budget."

Linking Verbs

A **linking verb** links the subject to a noun or adjective in the predicate. It must agree with the subject. A linking verb does not express action. Some common present-tense linking verbs are *am, are,* and *is.* Some common past-tense linking verbs are *was* and *were.*

*Carlos **is** an artist. His exhibits last year **were** beautiful.*

Your Turn Write each sentence. Underline each linking verb.

1. This painting is my favorite.
2. The colors are bright and joyful.
3. Carlos is proud of his most recent work.
4. I am anxious to see it.
5. Was he happy with the review on the Web?

Irregular Verbs

An **irregular verb** is a verb that does not end in -ed to form the past tense. Some also have special spellings when used with the helping verb *have*.

Present	Past	With *Have*
begin	began	begun
bring	brought	brought
come	came	come
do	did	done
draw	drew	drawn
eat	ate	eaten
give	gave	given
go	went	gone
grow	grew	grown
hide	hid	hidden
run	ran	run
say	said	said
see	saw	seen
sing	sang	sung
sit	sat	sat
take	took	taken
tell	told	told
think	thought	thought
write	wrote	written

Your Turn Write each sentence. Use the correct form of the verb in parentheses.

1. Last night I (go) to a spelling bee.
2. I (tell) my friend to meet me there.
3. We have (see) several spelling bees together.

Pronouns

Pronouns

A **pronoun** is a word that takes the place of one or more nouns. A **subject pronoun** is used as the subject of a verb. It tells who or what does the action. The pronouns *I, you, he, she, it, we,* and *they* can be used as subject pronouns.

An **object pronoun** is used as the object of a verb. It tells whom or what received the action of the verb. The pronouns *me, you, him, her, it, us,* and *them* can be used as object pronouns.

An object pronoun may come after prepositions such as *for, at, of, with,* or *to.*

*I gave **him** the hammer. **He** used **it** to build a shelf for **her**.*

Your Turn Write each sentence. Underline each subject pronoun. Circle each object pronoun.

1. She took the little statues out of the boxes.
2. Then she placed them on the new shelves.
3. They looked much better to her.
4. We went over to see what she had done.
5. You and he should invite her to dinner.

Pronoun-Antecedent Agreement

A **pronoun** must match its **antecedent**, the noun to which it refers. The antecedent may or may not be in the same sentence.

***Mom** said **she** knew what to do. **She** called my **brother** and gave **him** advice.*

Your Turn Write each sentence. Underline each pronoun. Circle each antecedent.

1. My brother asked Mom to drive him to work.
2. Dad printed the directions and gave them to Mom.
3. Dad was worried about my brother. He asked to go along.
4. Dad and Mom told my brother to expect them soon.

463

Reflexive Pronouns

A **reflexive pronoun** tells about an action that a subject does for or to itself. A reflexive pronoun is based on an object pronoun because it receives the action of the verb. The ending *-self* is added for singular pronouns. The ending *-selves* is added for plural pronouns.

*The girl wrote **herself** a note. We drove **ourselves** to the city.*

Your Turn Write each sentence. Underline only the reflexive pronoun(s).

1. We got ourselves lost in the city.
2. I asked myself how it happened.
3. You never expect to find yourself in trouble.
4. Trouble can find you all by itself.
5. My sister cheered for herself when she found a map.

Pronoun-Verb Agreement

A present-tense verb must **agree** with its subject, even if the subject is a pronoun.

*I **am** thirsty. She **is** thirsty. We **are** thirsty.*

Your Turn Write each sentence. Use the correct present-tense form of the verb in parentheses.

1. He (look) for a water fountain.
2. She (find) one over by the tennis courts.
3. We (proceed) from there to the parking lot.
4. Our parents beep the horn when they (see) us.
5. She (climb) into the front seat and (say), "Let's go!"

Possessive Pronouns

A **possessive pronoun** takes the place of a possessive noun. It shows who or what owns something. *My, your, her, his, its, our,* and *their* are possessive pronouns.

> *I gave **my** order to **our** waiter. He wrote it on **his** pad.*

Some possessive pronouns can stand on their own. *Mine, yours, hers, his, its, ours,* and *theirs* can be used alone.

> *We order lunch. I won't eat **mine** until **yours** is here.*

Your Turn Write each sentence. Replace the words in parentheses with a possessive pronoun.

1. (My friend Lauren's) sandwich looked very tasty.
2. Hers had more peppers than (the sandwich belonging to me).
3. "Can I have a bite of (the sandwich belonging to you)?" she asked.

Pronouns and Homophones

Some possessive pronouns sound like pronoun-verb contractions but are spelled differently. A possessive pronoun does not contain an apostrophe because no letters are missing.

> ***It's** time for the class to take **its** test. (**It's** = It + is; **its** is a possessive pronoun)*
>
> ***You're** proud of **your** grade. (**You're** = You + are; **your** is a possessive pronoun)*
>
> ***They're** not pleased with **their** grades. (**They're** = They + are; **their** is a possessive pronoun)*
>
> ***There's** no excuse for **theirs**. (**There's** = There + is; **theirs** is a possessive pronoun)*

Your Turn Write each sentence. Choose the correct word in parentheses to complete the sentence.

1. "You're not going to believe (you're, your) eyes," I said.
2. "(Theirs, There's) a B on my report card."
3. "Is it moving (it's, its) wings?" you asked.

Adjectives

Adjectives

An **adjective** describes a noun. Adjectives can tell **what kind** or **how many**. Most adjectives come directly before the nouns they describe. When an adjective comes after the noun it describes, the noun and adjective are connected by a **linking verb**.
A **proper adjective** is formed from a proper noun.

> My *two favorite* players on the team are *Brazilian*.

Your Turn Write each sentence. Circle each adjective and underline the noun being described.

1. We can't play on the wet fields.
2. The grass is slippery.

Articles

The words *the, a,* and *an* are special adjectives called **articles**. Use *a* before words that begin with consonant sounds. Use *an* before words that begin with vowel sounds.

> *A* squirrel dropped *the* acorns from *an* oak tree.

Your Turn Write the sentence. Circle each article.

1. The acorns clattered on the tin roof of an old garage.

This, That, These and *Those*

This, that, these and *those* are special adjectives that tell **how many** and **how near or far away** something or someone is. *This* (near) and *that* (far) are used with singular nouns. *These* (near) and *those* (far) are used with plural nouns.

> *These* apples in my hand came from *that* tree by the fence.

Your Turn Write the sentence. Choose the correct word in parentheses to complete the sentence.

1. We picked (that, these) apples from (this, those) tree.

Adjectives That Compare

Add **-er** to an adjective to compare two nouns. Add **-est** to compare more than two nouns.

If an adjective ends in a consonant and *y*, then change the *y* to *i* before adding *-er* or *-est*.

If an adjective ends in *e*, then drop the *e* before adding *-er* or *-est*.

If an adjective has a single vowel before a final consonant, then double the final consonant before adding *-er* or *-est*.

*I take the **lighter, tinier** box. The other box is the **thinnest** of all.*

Your Turn Write each sentence. Use the correct form of the adjective in parentheses.

1. My room is (big) than my sister's room.
2. "It's the (messy) room in the house!" Mom said.

Comparing: *More* and *Most, Good* and *Bad*

Use **more, better**, and **worse** to compare two people, places, or things.

Use **most, best,** and **worst** to compare more than two people, places, or things.

*I have **many** coins. You have **more** coins than I do. He has the **most** coins of all.*

*Eli is a **good** chef. Pam is a **better** chef than Eli. Chad is the **best** chef of all.*

*She had a **bad** day. He had a **worse** day than she did. I had the **worst** day of all.*

Use **more** and **most** with longer adjectives instead of adding the endings *-er* and *-est*.

*Mom had a **more pleasant** trip than I did. Dad had the **most exciting** trip of all.*

Your Turn Write each sentence. Use the correct form of the adjective in parentheses.

1. This restaurant has the (good) soup in town.
2. There were (many) choices today than yesterday.

467

Adverbs

Adverbs

An **adverb** is a word that tells more about a verb. Adverbs often tell *how, when,* or *where.* Many adverbs end in *-ly.*

You **nervously** looked **up**. The storm would start **soon**.

Your Turn Write each sentence. Circle each adverb and draw a line under the verb that each adverb describes.

1. Clouds gathered overhead.
2. Lightning flashed and thunder rumbled loudly.
3. We quickly raced inside.
4. "Is everyone here?" our father asked.
5. You quietly hoped the storm would go away.

Using *Good* and *Well*

Good is an adjective that tells more about a noun. **Well** is an adverb that is tells more about a verb.

The **good** nurse treated us **well**.

Your Turn Write each sentence. Choose *good* or *well* to complete the sentence. Underline the word that is being described.

1. There is a (good, well) chance that we will miss the play.
2. My mother did not sleep (good, well).
3. When I am sick, I can't perform (good, well).
4. Do you have any (good, well) suggestions?
5. A (good, well) actor might pretend to be healthy.

Adverbs That Compare

Adverbs can be used to compare two or more actions. Use *more* before most adverbs to compare two actions. Use *most* before most adverbs to compare more than two actions. Add the ending *-er* or *-est* to shorter adverbs to compare actions.

> Gil danced **longer** and **more gracefully** than Wendy.
> Shawna danced **longest** and **most gracefully** of all.

Your Turn Write each sentence. Choose the correct form of the adverb in parentheses.

1. Gil can move (swiftly) than Wendy.
2. Shawna works (hard) than Wendy.
3. Wendy learns new dances (fast) of all.
4. Have you danced (recently) than Gil?
5. Shawna has performed (consistently) of all the dancers.

Comparing with Irregular Adverbs

With the adverb **well**, use **better** to compare two actions. Use **best** to compare more than two actions.
With the adverb **badly**, use **worse** to compare two actions. Use **worst** to compare more than two actions.

> He and I played worse than yesterday, but you played best of all.

Your Turn Write each sentence. Choose the correct form of the adverb in parentheses.

1. I ran (well) at this race than the last one.
2. You had prepared (well) of all.
3. He reacted (badly) to the score than I did.
4. Their coach behaved (badly) of all.
5. Our coach understands the game (well) than any other coach.

469

Negatives

Negatives and Negative Contractions

A **negative** is a word that means *no*. Many negatives contain the word *no* within them. Some negatives use the contraction *n't*, which is short for *not*.

> **Nobody** wants to go first. I **can't** understand why.

Your Turn Write each sentence. Underline the negative word in each one.

1. We could not see anything inside the room.
2. There was no light switch on the wall.
3. I don't like going into a dark room.
4. I never enter a room that isn't lit brightly.
5. The lamps were nowhere to be found.

Double Negatives

Do not use two negatives in one sentence.

> *Don't you (**ever**, never) talk to me like that!*
> *I don't think (no one, **anyone**) should behave that way.*

Your Turn Write each sentence. Choose the correct word in parentheses to complete the sentence.

1. No one has (never, ever) won an argument with my mother.
2. We didn't have (no, any) idea what to say to her.
3. She won't take (any, none) of our advice.
4. Nothing (will, won't) make her change her mind.
5. Won't she trust (no one, anyone) other than herself?

Prepositions

Prepositions

A **preposition** comes before a noun or a pronoun. A preposition shows how the noun or pronoun is linked to another word in the sentence. Some common prepositions are *in, at, of, from, with, to,* and *by.*

   The conductor **on** the train waved **at** the boy.

Your Turn Write each sentence. Circle each preposition.

1. He gave his ticket to the conductor.
2. The train left from the station at noon.
3. He sat by the window with his mother.
4. The motion of the train shook his belongings.
5. The book with the blue cover fell from his backpack.

Prepositional Phrases

A **prepositional phrase** is a group of words that begins with a preposition and ends with a noun or pronoun. The noun or pronoun is the **object of the preposition**. A prepositional phrase can be used as an adjective or an adverb in a sentence.

   The girl **in the park** (adjective) hit the ball **over the net** (adverb).

Your Turn Write each sentence. Underline each prepositional phrase and circle each preposition. Then place an "O" above the object of the preposition.

1. The ball bounced at her feet.
2. The girl with the long hair kept score.
3. They played for three hours.
4. My friend and I cheered from the bleachers.
5. My favorite one of the players scored the last point.

471

Mechanics: Abbreviations

Titles and Names

Some titles are **abbreviations,** or shortened forms of words. Other titles, like *Ms.* and *Mrs.,* don't have longer forms. An **initial** is the first letter of a name. Titles and initials are capitalized and are followed by a period. When abbreviations are used at the end of an Internet address, they are not capitalized or followed by a period.

Dr. A. J. Moreno will post Sen. Paulsen's speech on our state's .gov Web site.

Your Turn Write each sentence. Change the word(s) in parentheses into an abbreviation or initial.

1. I sent an e-mail to (Mister) Elish.
2. (Governor) Slater also wrote a response.
3. Ms. (Carol Jane) Stein will speak to our class next week.
4. I posted the news at www.ourschool.(educational) today.
5. Let's give a warm welcome to (Doctor) and (his wife) Yee.

Time

Use abbreviations to indicate time before noon (A.M. for "ante meridiem") and after noon (P.M. for "post meridiem"). These abbreviations are capitalized with periods after each letter.

*Our car wash will go from 10 **A.M.** to 2 **P.M.** on Saturday.*

Your Turn Write each sentence. Use the correct abbreviation to replace the words in parentheses.

1. We will take a break for lunch at 12:30 (after noon).
2. I don't have to be there until 11:00 (before noon).
3. The dog usually waits until 7:30 (in the morning) to wake me up.
4. Mom will pick us up at 2:30 (in the afternoon).
5. I'll be able to walk the dog at 8:00 (in the evening).

Days and Months

When you abbreviate the **days of the week** or the **months of the year**, begin with a capital letter and end with a period. Do not abbreviate *May, June,* or *July.*

Sun.   Mon.   Tues.   Wed.   Thurs.   Fri.   Sat.

Jan.   Feb.   Mar.   Apr.   Aug.   Sept.   Oct.   Nov.   Dec.

Your Turn Write each sentence. Use the correct abbreviation(s) to replace the word(s) in parentheses.

1. I have a piano lesson each (Tuesday) in July.
2. Soccer practice only goes until (November) this year.
3. The drama club uses the theater each (Monday) in (March) for rehearsals.
4. The final production begins in (April) and runs until (June).
5. I've blocked out (Wednesday) through (Friday) for vacation.

Addresses

Address abbreviations are capitalized and followed by a period. Some common address abbreviations are **St.** (Street), **Rd.** (Road), **Ave.** (Avenue), **Dr.** (Drive), **Blvd.** (Boulevard), **Ln.** (Lane), **Apt.** (Apartment), and **P. O.** (Post Office), When you write an address, you may use United States Postal Service abbreviations for the names of states. All of these abbreviations are two capital letters with no period at the end. When using these state abbreviations, no comma is needed after the name of the city or town.

*She mailed the postcard to 28 Irving **Dr.**, **Apt.** 4B, Canton **OH**.*

Your Turn Write each address. Use the correct abbreviation(s) whenever possible.

1. 6 Main Street
2. Post Office Box 1023
3. Providence, Rhode Island
4. 532 Jefferson Street, Los Angeles, California
5. 104 7th Avenue, Apartment 8C, New York, New York

Mechanics: Capitalization

First Words in Sentences

Capitalize the first word of a sentence. Capitalize the first word of a direct quotation. Do not capitalize the second part of an interrupted quotation. When the second part of a quotation is a new sentence, put a period after the interrupting expression and capitalize the first word of the new sentence.

"Finish your homework," my mother said, "and come down for supper."

Dinner smelled great. "I'll be right there," I replied. "I'm almost done."

Your Turn **Write each sentence. Use capital letters correctly.**

1. the final problem was taking a long time to answer.
2. "did you hear what I said?" asked my mother.
3. without looking up, I replied, "yes, I did."
4. "don't wait too long," Mom said, "or it will get cold."
5. "this is too hard," I said. "maybe I can finish it later."

Letter Greetings and Closings

All of the words in a letter's greeting begin with a capital letter. Only the first word in the closing of a letter begins with a capital letter.

Dear Dr. Watkins, Sincerely yours,

Your Turn **Write each part of a letter with the correct capitalization.**

1. dear uncle floyd,
2. best wishes
3. with all my love,
4. dear ladies and gentlemen,
5. to whom it may concern:

Proper Nouns: Names and Titles of People

Capitalize the names of people and the initials that stand for their names. Capitalize titles or abbreviations of titles when they come before or after the names of people. Capitalize words that show family relationships when used as titles or as substitutes for a person's name. Do not capitalize words that show family relationships when they are preceded by a possessive noun or pronoun. Capitalize the pronoun *I*.

> *Dean's father and I talked to Mom about his visit to*
> *Dr. T. J. Hunter, Jr.*

Your Turn Write each sentence. Use capital letters correctly.

1. mr. weston worried about Dean's swollen knee.
2. "I'll ask dad what to do about it," Dean had told me.
3. "What did dr. hunter tell him?" i asked my mother.
4. "He was sent to another doctor," mom explained.

Titles of Works

Capitalize the first, last, and all important words in the title of a book, play, short story, poem, movie, article, newspaper, magazine, TV series, chapter of a book, or song.

> *My father sang "Moon River" while I watched "Alice in*
> *Wonderland" again.*
> *The book* Give Us a Chance *was reviewed in today's*
> Tarrytown Tribune.

Your Turn Write each sentence. Use capital letters correctly.

1. We sang "america the beautiful" at the start of the game.
2. A reporter from the hometown herald wrote about it.
3. He compared the victory to the movie "the miracle team."
4. I wrote a poem about it called "winning by the book."

Other Proper Nouns and Adjectives

Capitalize the names of cities, states, countries, and continents. Do not capitalize articles or prepositions that are part of the names. Capitalize the names of bodies of water and geographical features. Capitalize the names of sections of the country. Do not capitalize compass points when they just show direction.

Portland, Oregon   California is south of the Pacific Northwest.

Capitalize the names of streets and highways. Capitalize the names of buildings, bridges, and monuments.

Mackinaw Bridge   Empire State Building

Capitalize the names of stars and planets. Capitalize *Earth* when it refers to the planet. Do not capitalize *earth* when it is preceded by the article *the*. Do not capitalize *sun* or *moon*.

The planet next closest to the sun from the earth is Venus.

Capitalize the names of schools, clubs, teams, businesses, and products.

Junior Debate Club at Westwood Senior High School

Capitalize the names of historic events, periods of time, and documents.

the Battle of Bunker Hill   the Declaration of Independence

Capitalize the days of the week, months of the year, and holidays.

Labor Day is the first Monday in September.

Capitalize the names of ethnic groups, nationalities, and languages. Capitalize proper adjectives that are formed from the names of ethnic groups and nationalities.

The official languages of the Swiss include German and French.

Capitalize the first word of each main topic and subtopic in an outline.

1. Products and exports
*   A. Natural resources*

Mechanics: Punctuation

End Punctuation

A **declarative sentence** makes a statement. It ends with a **period (.)**.

An **interrogative sentence** asks a question. It ends with a **question mark (?)**.

An **imperative sentence** makes a command or a request. It ends with a **period (.)** or an **exclamation mark (!)**.

An **exclamatory sentence** expresses strong emotion. It ends with an **exclamation mark (!)**.

Do you like trapeze artists? Watch how daring they are! I'm afraid of heights like that.

Your Turn **Write each sentence. Use the correct capitalization and end punctuation.**

1. When is the next performance
2. Get tickets now before they sell out
3. I can't wait to see the fire-breathing acrobats
4. Her plane flies east from chicago on valentine's day.

Periods

Use a period at the end of an abbreviation. Use a period in abbreviations for time. Use a period after initials. Use a period after numbers and letters in an outline.

Dr. E. J. Simmons will see us at 4:45 P.M. on Feb. 23.

Your Turn **Write each sentence. Insert periods where needed.**

1. I would prefer an appointment at 10:00 AM.
2. Ms Etchells has scheduled the test for Oct 5.
3. My best friend, B D Shea, will park at Elm St and wait.
4. Is 7:30 PM too late for Dr West to see you?

Colons and Semicolons

Use a **colon** to separate the hour and minute when you write the time of day. Use a colon after the greeting of a business letter. Use a **semicolon** to combine two related independent clauses that are not connected by a conjunction such as *or, and,* or *but.*

> *Dear Professor Cooper:*
> *I cannot make your 10:30 class today; our cat is sick.*

Your Turn Write each sentence. Insert the proper punctuation where it is needed.

1. Dear Mr. Kirov
2. I tried to call you this morning no one answered the phone.

Apostrophes

Use an **apostrophe (')** and an *s* to form the possessive of a singular noun. Use an apostrophe and an *s* to form the possessive of a plural noun that does not end in *s.* Use an apostrophe alone to form the possessive of a plural noun that ends in *s.* Do not use an apostrophe in a possessive pronoun. Use an apostrophe in a **contraction** to show where a letter or letters are missing.

> *My **friend's** family **didn't** borrow a car because **theirs** was fixed.*

Parentheses

Use parentheses to set off information that is not essential in a sentence, such as unnecessary details, clarifications, or examples.

> *Jim (winner of last year's contest) didn't register for this year.*

Your Turn Write each sentence. Insert apostrophes and parentheses where needed.

1. This years entry fee $25 last year shouldnt increase.
2. Our familys car over 10 years old is very reliable.

Commas

Use a **comma (,)** between the name of a city and the complete name of a state. Use a comma after the name of a state or a country when it is used with the name of a city in a sentence. Do not use a comma between the name of a city and the postal service abbreviation for a state.

We drove from Houston, Texas, to Toronto, Canada, in one week.

Use a **comma** between the day and the year in a date. Use a comma before and after the year when it is used with both the month and the day in a sentence. Do not use a comma if only the month and the year are given.

We gathered on August 5, 1987, for our last reunion.

Use a **comma** after the greeting in a friendly letter and after the closing in all letters.

Dear Aunt Jo,   Very truly yours,

Use a **comma** before *and, but,* or *or* when it joins simple sentences to form a compound sentence. Use a comma to separate two or more subjects in a compound subject. Use a comma to separate two or more predicates in a compound predicate and after a dependent clause at the start of a sentence.

After the bell rang, Liz, Jack, and Chris left, but I remained.

Use a **comma** to set off a direct quotation.

"When you heard the bell," she asked, "had you finished the test?"

Use **commas** to separate three or more items in a series.

She photographed the roses, lilies, and orchids on display.

Use a **comma** after the words *yes* or *no* or other introductory words at the beginning of a sentence. Use a comma with nouns in a direct address.

Yes, I know Brady. By the way, Donna, have you talked to him?

Your Turn Write each sentence. Add commas where needed.

1. The residents of Smith South Carolina wanted a town flag.
2. I submitted six drawings but none of them were chosen.

Quotation Marks

Use **quotation marks** before and after the exact words that a speaker says or writes. Use a **comma** or **commas** to separate a clause, such as *he said*, from the quotation itself. Place the comma outside the opening quotation marks but inside the closing quotation marks. Place a **period** inside closing quotation marks. Place a **question mark** or **exclamation mark** inside the quotation marks when it is part of the quotation.

> *"Did you finish your assignment?" my mother asked.*
> *"I started it," I replied, "but my baby brother interrupted me."*

Use **quotation marks** around the title of a short story, song, short poem, print or online article, or chapter of a book.

> *I wrote a poem called "My Bratty Baby Brother."*

Your Turn Write each sentence. Add quotation marks where needed.

1. Our school journal published My Bratty Baby Brother.
2. What gave you the idea for that poem? my teacher asked.
3. It can be so frustrating at home sometimes! I said.

Italics (Underlining)

Use italics or underlining for the title of a book, movie, television series, play, stage production, magazine, or newspaper.

> *We had tickets to see* <u>The Lion King</u> *in August.*

Your Turn Write each sentence. Underline titles where needed.

1. I borrowed The Big Book of Ballet from the library.
2. We had just watched The Company on television.